A CATS
a century of tradition

Painting by Virginia Perle.

Gary Jobson and Roy Wilkins

nomad press

DEDICATION

To Nelson Hartranft, for his vision keeping the A Cat class alive.

Nomad Press

A division of Nomad Communications

10 9 8 7 6 5 4 3 2 1

ISBN: 0-9749344-7-x

Questions regarding the ordering of this book should be addressed to

Independent Publishers Group

814 N. Franklin St.

Chicago, IL 60610

www.ipgbook.com

Nomad Press

2456 Christian St.

White River Junction, VT 05001

www.nomadpress.net

CONTENTS

A perfect start as the A Cat fleet heads upwind. In any given race every boat has a chance to win.

Fair Wind My Friend

Be fair to wet boards and rolling beam.
Be kind to crisp white sail, so tightly seamed.
Lift me like sweet breeze beneath gliding wings of hawks,
and swing me around far glistening marks.

Caress me bow to stern and feel my pounding heart.
Shove me not to shore or shoal; sweep me 'round to distant start
where winning horn and whistles wait and call;
where fellow sailors cheer A Cat fleet, one and all.

Chetra E. Kotzas

FOREWORD

Downwind, as you can imagine, an A Cat is a little interesting. Trying to jibe them is more than interesting.

—Peter Kellogg

When one sees the big, beautiful A Cats sailing, one can't help wanting to be a part of all that. I was first inspired as a child watching these magnificent boats sail. At the age of 18, I bought a share of the A Cat, *Lotus*, with a friend, David McShane.

These boats are unique to Barnegat Bay, having been specifically designed to take into account the bay's ample wind and shallow waters, and they have become a tradition here. In most classes, when someone asks who won a race, the name of the skipper is generally mentioned. Because the A Cats have such a history, when people talk about the day's results, they use the name of the boat rather than the name of the skipper.

I suggested to Gary Jobson and Roy Wilkins that they collaborate on a book about our class. They both grew up sailing on Barnegat Bay. As the A Cat fleet captain, Roy has been instrumental in making the class grow and prosper. With his local and international knowledge, Gary brings a terrific perspective to the project.

The following work is a wonderful collection of the past and current history of the fleet, the yacht clubs from which they sail, and the trophies for which they race.

I hope this volume encourages the junior sailors on Barnegat Bay and the Ocean County College Sailing Team to sail A Cats in future years. I also hope it rekindles special memories for those who have either sailed or admired these amazing boats in the past.

Peter Kellogg
August 2005

Torch *blasts to windward. Like all A Cats, she has plenty of windward helm.*

THE GRAND YACHTS OF BARNEGAT BAY

Painting by John English.

Even from a distance, the four sails approaching were impressive. The year was 1958 and I watched from the Beachwood Yacht Club dock as the *Bat*, the *Spy*, the *Lotus*, and the *Mary Ann* raced for the finish line between the Crabbe's *Gulf Steam* and barrel 17.

When the grand yachts closed, a crowd formed as everyone stopped to enjoy the finish. The race was close. Sailors waist deep in the water hauling out their sneakboxes, scows, or Jet 14s stood on their toes to get a better look. Saturday afternoon strollers over on the boardwalk, swimmers in the water, and kids eating ice cream at the old pavilion all stopped whatever they were doing to witness the A Cat finish.

To an eight-year-old used to crewing on a 10-foot Toms River pram, the mighty A Cats looked gigantic. The usual southeasterly was blowing at least 18 knots. I can still remember the bow waves foaming while the crews all sat well aft, and when they got close I could see the intensity on the faces of the crews. Each main trimmer worked hard as two boats started a luffing match. The stakes were high: the winner would claim the coveted rooster flag for the next week.

As the four A Cats made their final sprint it came right down to the wire, because the trailing boats blocked the wind of the leaders. Everyone was screaming. The two luffers sailed by the lee as they bore off. The BBYRA race committee fired the cannon and the crowd cheered. *Lotus* took it. Within seconds all four boats were finished, and then they turned up into the wind making graceful, sweeping, arching turns to avoid running aground or hitting the dock where I was standing. The helmsmen pushed the tillers hard. Halyards were prepared for lowering the sails and anchors appeared out of the cabin. The sails luffed furiously as the boats pointed directly into the wind. Burly foredeck crew heaved the anchors, the mains dropped, the booms fell naturally into their wooden crutches, and suddenly, all was quiet.

The crowd returned to their activities. When the three losers let out a spontaneous hip-hip-hurray for the *Lotus*, I asked my father why the cheers? He told me, "sportsmanship is important."

Growing up on Barnegat Bay, I raced prams, penguins, M Scows, sneakboxes, duckboats, diamonds, Jet 14s, Flying Scots, lightnings, blue jays, auxiliaries, and the speedy E Scows. However, no matter what boat I might be sailing, the A Cats always captured my attention. My view of the A Cats was usually from the deck of an E Scow, where I crewed as a teenager with the legendary Sam Merrick. The A Cats were right there, sharing the same course with us. I remember someone referring to the seven C's: Colie, Campbell, Chance, Chapman, Carson, Crabbe and Cox. They were the heroes of the day on Barnegat Bay.

Occasionally, I was invited to actually race on an A Cat. I'll never forget being aboard the *Bat* during a jibe off Good Luck Point. The boom and sail swung across with great force. Somehow the backstay was not pulled in on time and the mast snapped and fell right into the water.

Over the years I have been lucky to sail on the waters of every continent, including Antarctica, and I've sailed with many of the world's most gifted sailors. My most cherished sailing memories include

Fred Winkelman displays his many trophies in the 1950s. Notice the classic car and powerboat in the background. The A Cat, however, is ageless.

Spy, Mary Ann, Lotus, *and* Bat *in a tight race off Seaside Park. It is interesting that the leech tension on the lead boat seems tighter than on the trailing boats. Could this be the difference?*

battling the monster seas during the 1979 Fastnet Race, watching *Australia II* pass *Liberty* in the final race of the 1983 America's Cup, rounding Cape Horn, winning the America's Cup with Ted Turner aboard *Courageous*, and that awe-inspiring finish of the A Cats when I was only eight years old.

I was thrilled when a new A Cat was built in 1980, followed by three more by the end of the '90s. These boats are a vital tie to Barnegat Bay's historical roots, and they had been threatened with extinction. During that time I was racing maxi boats all over the world but I kept in touch with my Barnegat Bay friends about the revitalized A Cat class. It makes me smile thinking about all the pride generated

by these magnificent, single-sail boats. The fleet is certainly competitive and winning is important, but just being part of the fleet is an honor.

When Peter Kellogg first suggested writing a book on A Cats, I was enthused. Images from the past filled my head. Unfortunately, illness kept me from working on the project, but once I recovered, the year-long delay only increased my determination to document the boat and its proud history.

Peter suggested that I work with Roy Wilkins, who I found to be one of the most enthusiastic promoters of sailing in America. Together, Roy and I took on this project, which I at first thought would be a history book. But after talking with lots of Barnegat Bay sailors, I realized that the golden age of A Cat sailing is taking place during our lifetime. Who better than the owners and crews themselves to tell this story? Through the winter months I interviewed dozens of A Cat denizens. It was most enjoyable to lob a question and sit back and listen as the stories of the sailors just spilled out into my tape machine. Through the process we generated hundreds of pages of material.

Over the years I've sailed on five America's Cup teams and covered six more cups for ESPN. As a result, I look at the world's oldest, continuously held sporting event with wide eyes. The participants put everything they have into winning, so it can be an emotional rollercoaster ride. I can report from experience it is a lot more fun being on a winning boat than a losing boat. As a journalist I'm fascinated how sailors talk about their experiences and by the passion sailing instills in them. I discovered that the profile of an A Cat sailor is no different from that of an America's Cup competitor.

Decades from now I bet the sailors of tomorrow won't be any different from the sailors of today. After researching the history of the A Cat races dating back to 1871 (only one year after the first

Every crew seems to have an important job in this up-bay versus down-bay rivalry.

America's Cup defense in New York Harbor), I found the present-day A Cat events very similar to the regattas of yesteryear.

Our goal in *A Cats: A Century of Tradition* is to let the sailors tell their stories, and combined with beautiful photographs and artwork, to record this amazing age of the A Cats for our enjoyment and for the sailors of the future.

Gary Jobson

July 2005

A HISTORY OF A CATS

Painting by Virginia Perle.

It's no accident that boats evolve from the waters they ply. The Scandinavians designed long, narrow boats to battle choppy seas, Dutch boats use lee boards on flat-bottom hulls to sail shallow waters, and the Polynesians created multihulls to swiftly travel from island to island. The mariners of Barnegat Bay needed sturdy boats to move cargo across its choppy waters. Single-sail catboats were powerful vessels that could handle heavy loads, and while big sails were a handful, they were necessary to make good time, efficient in both strong or light winds.

Being first to bring goods to market or deliver passengers has always been a priority for profit-minded entrepreneurs. And racing for almost any reason is part of the fabric of human nature. It was inevitable that the workboats of Barnegat Bay would compete.

With the advent of the railroads prosperous people could move easily, and like today, the "Jet Set" of the 1800s wanted to go to the sea. Elaborate resorts along the Jersey Shore attracted the well-to-do from Philadelphia. Along popular rail routes, yacht clubs were formed in Bay Head, Seaside Park, and Island Heights. Sailing the workboats became sport. It didn't take long for owners and skippers to strive to sail faster, a passion that continues to drive the A Cat sailors of today.

Nice period attire on a summer day at Island Heights Yacht Club.

Barnegat Bay and the Catboat

This shallow body of water, about 40 miles long, bordered by the New Jersey coastline on the west and the narrow barrier beach to the east, runs from the Mallica River in the south to the Metedeconk River in the north. The first written report of the bay comes from author Robert Juet, traveling with explorer Henry Hudson in 1609: "We came to a great lake of water, as we could judge it to be . . . the mouth of that lake hath many shoals and the sea breaketh upon them as it is cast out of

Crowds always form when the A Cats race. This might have been a popular postcard (circa 1925).

the mouth of it . . . This is a very good land to fall in with, and a pleasant land to see."

Dutch captain Cornelius Mey is credited with naming the inlet "Barendegat," which translates as "breaking inlet," due to the rough conditions where the bay meets the Atlantic. Inlets have opened and closed through the years, but the long, shallow

The crews all wear ties during the race. (l–r) Spy, Mary Ann, Bat, *and* Helen, *1924.*

My first A Cat experience would have been on Mary Ann. *I was about five years old, and I think the owner might have been Mary and Bob Byrns. They had me down below passing out beers, which, of course, fueled the crew to a few victories. That was my job—pumping and passing out beer. There was a considerable amount of water in the boat at that time, too. It wasn't like they are now today. They are so dry now you can get a coughing spell from dust. Totally different.*

—Snapper Applegate, son of Brit Applegate

bay was home to Native Americans and, later, a succession of settlers.

The early settlers took advantage of the native white cedar to build watercraft, a necessary means of transportation along the bay with all its coves, estuaries, islands, and marshes. Life on Barnegat Bay was not that difficult. Natural resources abounded, food was easy to come by, the pleasures of the bay and the ocean beaches were close at hand. The woods and marshes provided salt, hay, and timber. Glass was made from the ubiquitous sand, and the bogs provided soft iron. And then there were the bay's own riches: plentiful fish, seafood, and waterfowl. But one needed a boat to move around. The timber had to be felled and hauled to various mills, and fish and seafood had to be caught and brought to port. A special kind of boat was needed to operate in the shoal waters of Barnegat

There is always a sense of anticipation around the docks before a race. Sailors like to study each other to see if they can find an edge even before setting sail.

Bay. They were generally wide, low, and stable, allowing for the transportation of passengers, timber, seafood, and other goods. These boats eventually became known as "catboats," possibly derived from portholes in the forward part of the hull that resemble cat eyes. The low freeboard makes them look like cats lying in the grass.

In the 1830s, Hazelton Seaman is credited with building the first Barnegat Bay sneakbox, a type of catboat, in West Creek. This small, extremely shallow-draft vessel was well-suited to navigating shoal waters and marshy coves. It was easily covered with camouflage for hunters. The first example was called a "devil's coffin."

In the early 1900s, J.H. Perrine began building sneakboxes in Barnegat. The sneakboxes were also daysailed purely for pleasure and raced competitively.

The Leisure Class and Racing

Once the railroad opened Barnegat Bay to summer visitors from New York and Philadelphia, names like Rockefeller, Vanderbilt, Gould, Astor, Kipp, Rhinelander, and Wanamaker were heard more and more in the little villages.

By 1871, there were enough sailboats informally racing on Barnegat Bay to prompt the town of Toms River to organize the Toms River Challenge Cup and to create the Toms River Yacht Club to host the race. Captains and crews of boats that plied their trades along the coast took great pleasure in out-sailing each other. Wagering was prevalent, and passions ran high during these races.

A suitable trophy for the Toms River Challenge Cup, a 3.5-pound ornate silver "mug" with an anchor and line on the handles, was made by Tiffany & Company for the enormous sum of $175. This is the

Lotus *circa 1931, Edwin Schoettle family.*

place at exactly 10 in the morning. Boats would draw for their positions on the line, and maintain a certain distance between them.

The trophy was hotly contested from the beginning. It was reported that armed guards stood watch to protect against night raids by other competitors. It all sounds similar to the atmosphere surrounding the America's Cup of today.

Eight gaff-rigged cats competed in that first race. *Vapor* won and she immediately received four challenges. The race committee met the next day and added a few rules, indicating there must have been fierce competition. For example, measurement protocols were initiated (there was the question of ratings even then). Catboats could only carry one sail, while sloops were permitted one jib and a mainsail. The Challenge Cup was raced again in October 1871, and *Vapor* won again.

second oldest American sailing trophy in continuous competition, second only to the America's Cup.

Rules for the July 27 race agreed that "the race would be open to all yachts with ownership not to have changed hands within three months of the event, and whose owners lived between Bay Head and Tuckertown." The anchored start was to take

The racing was reported to be quite evenly matched, despite the boats' design disparities.

Just before the turn of the last century, two boats changed the competition on the bay. Amos Lewis' *Bouquet*, a Carey Smith design, and Edwin Schoettle's *Scat*, a 26-foot Crosby Cat from Cape Cod by way of Long Island, brought new design

> *There is sort of an aura with the A Cats. It's one of the few boats you can have a large group of people on and still have competitiveness. The Challenge Cup was a big activity around here in the summer, before A Cats. Catboats were primarily workboats at that time, they would move cargo and gather clams and oysters. And then they got together to race. They usually had a captain who raced the boat for the owners in a much more formal way than nowadays. There was money involved, and they had to pay to race. It was $10. Back in those days, $10 was a lot of money, especially for around here because there really just wasn't much work outside of being a bay man.*
>
> —Alicemay Weber-Wright, lifelong A Cat sailor

ideas. In 1896 the working catboats were edged out of competition by these yachts designed to win races. The workboats couldn't compete with the newer "naval architect–designed" innovations.

The A Cat is Born

In 1922, Charles D. Mower, a well-respected boat designer, accepted a commission from Judge Charles McKeehan of Philadelphia to design a sailing vessel that would win the Toms River Challenge Cup, and specifically, to beat the gaff-rigged cat, *Virginia*, also designed by Mower. The result was the first A Cat on Barnegat Bay, the *Mary Ann*, built by Morton Johnson of Bay Head.

Mary Ann, named after Judge McKeehan's mother, was 28 feet long overall, 22 feet at the

Bat *and* Mary Ann *duel for the lead off Seaside Park.*

Race day, Island Heights Yacht Club, 1941.

her centerboard down she draws 6 feet, giving her serious biting-in capabilities to weather." The A Cats started with a "Swedish" rig, that is, with the main high on the hoist and a 9-foot gaff. Quickly, the gaff was retired in favor of a Marconi rig.

Mary Ann's mast, set well forward, towered 46 feet above the deck, with two shrouds on either side, three forestays, and running backstays. Her boom, at 28 feet, allowed for an enormous 615 square feet of sail area. She was built of native Barnegat Bay cedar on oak, fastened with bronze and copper. *Mary Ann* out-sailed the other contestants for the Toms River Challenge Cup in July 1922.

As a result of *Mary Ann's* success, within a year two more A Cats graced the bay. Ed Crabbe hired Mower and the Morton Johnson yard to create *Bat*, while Frank Thatcher built *Helen* at Hopper's Basin. *Helen* proved to be so slow that Thatcher did not race her a second season: he had *Spy* built in 1924 at the Morton Johnson yard, virtually identical to *Mary Ann*. *Helen* was probably destroyed. The last Mower/Johnson A Cat, *Lotus*, was built in 1925 for Bob Truitt.

Meanwhile, Francis Sweisguth, another well-respected designer who had done the Star boat

waterline, with a 12-foot beam. Historic accounts described the new boat as, "Not quite half as wide as long, but close. With her low freeboard and her shallow bilges, she draws two and a half feet, perfect for navigating shallow Barnegat Bay. *Mary Ann* has a large centerboard, and a substantial skeg, from which the underhung rudder depends. With

The view from the Schoettle homestead in Island Heights looking west at their new boat, Forcem *(circa 1923).*

I think the most amazing description is just the way it looks. It's 28 feet long, 12 feet wide and has a 48- or 50-foot mast. And then the boom is 28 feet long—the physical picture that it presents, especially if you are standing next to the sail, is just pretty amazing.
—Gary Stewart, owner of *Spy*

in 1911 based on a design by William Gardner, also drew two A Cat designs in 1923: *Tamwock* for Francis Larkin; and *Forcem* for Edwin Schoettle, Ed Harrington, and two other unknown partners. In contrast to the Mower design, which had a sloped bow, Sweisguth's plans called for a blunt bow. The skegs were also a bit different, but the cabin, cockpit, and sailplans were the same. Both *Tamwock* and *Forcem* were built by John Kirk. Susan Davis, the granddaughter of Edwin Shoettle, reports that *Forcem* was slow, and legend has it the boat was scuttled early in her life.

The Great Depression curtailed further expansion of the A Cat fleet, and *Tamwock* was destroyed in 1940 in a fire, leaving only four of the original seven A Cats sailing on the bay.

A Cats Revived

Nelson R. Hartranft was enchanted as a boy by the sight of these boats. There are many adjectives to describe them: exotic, bold, powerful, businesslike, graceful, and sleek. An A Cat makes one strong statement when you look at it. The bow looks ready to push away the choppy waves. It is no wonder that A Cat crews look so intense: the boat demands it.

In the 1970s, one by one Nelson bought all the existing A Cats, which by then had been subject to decades of decline. He had a plan: he was going to revive the class.

Nelson first bought *Lotus* in 1974. Then he rescued *Spy* in 1975 and *Bat* in 1976. In 1978, he bought *Mary Ann*. He worked with other A Cat enthusiasts to keep the boats sailing, helping with repairs and passing them on to others at modest prices as long as the new owners would agree to maintain and sail them.

Nelson wanted to build a new A Cat but he couldn't find any plans for the original boats. He tried to persuade Beaton's to build one, confident of their abilities to do so. Beaton's was not persuaded. Then, incredibly, a set of Francis Sweisguth's plans for *Tamwock* were found in a chest of drawers in an antique shop, enabling Hartranft to convince Lachlan "Lolly" Beaton to build a traditional A Cat. Beaton thought that would be a good experience for his son, Tom. And so the boat was built as it would have been decades before, using white oak, white cedar planking, and canvas on fir for the deck. The spars were built hollow, using spruce-staved construction, strong and lightweight. Tommy Beaton reflects,

Lotus. *Notice the unique white transom.*

The post-race scene at Enos, 1949. Were the sailors guests at the hotel as the sign on the left demands?

"For the size of the boat they are not difficult in a traditional sense, but they are a lot of work for a 28-foot boat. There's a lot of structure to support the mast that far forward." An A Cat takes 4,000 hours to complete. Nelson Hartranft's new boat was christened *Wasp* in 1980, and caused quite a stir on Barnegat Bay, being the first new A Cat since *Lotus* in 1925. Beaton went on to rebuild *Spy* and *Lotus*, and the *Mary Ann* and *Bat* were also rebuilt during this time. Pumping water out of the bilge was a tradition most A Cat owners wanted to retire permanently. Everyone expected that the last rebuilt boat performed the best.

Another resurgence in the class came when Peter Kellogg, once owner of the *Lotus* (1964–1971), re-caught the A Cat bug and asked John Brady, of the Philadelphia Maritime Museum, to build a traditional boat. Brady used the Mower plans, while Beaton was using Sweisguth's plans. It's ironic that Mower and Sweisguth are still competing 80 years later. Both would be proud to see their enduring designs performing so well.

One of the reasons the A Cats are still around is they are perfectly suited for racing on Barnegat Bay. They are as big a boat that is practical there. Using the crew for ballast makes it a social event as well as a race and I think that adds to it. The design concept is as good as it gets for racing in a shallow body of water.

—John Brady, builder of *Tamwock*, *Vapor*, *Spy II*, and *Torch*

The new Kellogg boat was christened *Tamwock* in honor of the original boat that had been lost in a fire. A previous owner, Al Diss, had been asked for his permission to revive the name. He

The crewman on the left seems to be doing pushups, or is he getting up for a tack? The proper term is "laying decks." The classic southeasterly is blowing 20 knots off Seaside in the 1950s. Charlie Lord's father is the gentleman in white forward of the cabin.

gave his approval, along with a treasure trove of memorabilia from the original *Tamwock*.

Beaton's built another Sweisguth-designed boat in 1994. William "Doc" Fortenbaugh's *Ghost* utilized modern building techniques, useful for go-fast racing, but not of the cut-throat variety. Fortenbaugh did very well with *Ghost*, giving the credit to Beaton's careful construction, his crew, and the fact that he didn't let water sit in the bilge. Tom Beaton, an accomplished sailor himself, gives as much credit to Fortenbaugh's skill on the water.

Meanwhile, Peter Kellogg had sold *Tamwock* and commissioned another A Cat, again by John Brady, who was now working for the Philadelphia Ship Preservation Guild. Go-fast was definitely on both their minds. *Vapor*, also launched in 1994, was named after the boat that won the first Toms River Challenge Cup in 1871.

These new boats were competing with the original A Cats, now nearly 80 years old. By 2000, *Spy* was once again giving the bailers hefty workouts. Owner Roy Wilkins didn't want to abandon the original Mower-designed boat, but wasn't sure that the boat could be competitive after another re-build. Peter Kellogg to the rescue! He had a plan: to buy *Spy* and donate her to the Toms River Seaport Museum, where she would be repaired and become an exhibit. Wilkins could then use the sale proceeds to pay John Brady, now at the Independence Seaport Museum, to build him a new A Cat, and Kellogg would make up the difference in cost. Wilkins agreed. Who wouldn't?

Brady recognized that this boat would be different from the others he'd built. He consciously set out to build a light boat, but not one that would "ruin the class." Launched for the 2001 season she was christened *Spy II* and, happily for Wilkins and partners Maggie Groff, Gary Stewart, and Richard Yetman, won the BBYRA Championship.

Yet another boat had joined the fleet that year, *Raven*, built by Beaton's for a syndicate of four. Dave Alldian, Pete Stagaard, Cory Wingerter, and Mike Tufariello, who had earlier bought the *Tamwock*, which proved to be slow, wanted a truly competitive boat.

Bat *tuning up with Schoettle's* Noisy Lady. *Their other boat was named* Silent Maid. *Interesting contrast.*

Strength for the Future

Time for a reality check amongst the owners. A Cats long held a sort of even trade-off between the boats. Everyone seemed to hit a winning streak every

Enos Restaurant, left, is the destination for Lotus *ghosting up the Forked River along the banks. You can taste the beer from here.*

now and then, but the advent of new construction methods and modern materials had demonstrably altered the playing field.

The owners decided to establish several new rules. Their one-design class, after all, had two designers and a variety of weights. The lightest was *Spy II* at 4,096 pounds, and the heaviest was *Tamwock* at 5,126 pounds, 25 percent heavier. Something had to be done. Minimum weights were set, and ballast stations assigned for the boats that were deemed too light. For future construction, rules were set as to the materials used. No "exotics" except for rudder and centerboard were allowed and minimum numbers of frames, both hull and deck, were decided. Sail composition and cut were standardized. Sailmakers were chosen who would provide the sails at a fixed rate.

The measurement adjustments worked. In 2003, seven out of ten A Cats won at least one race. In 2004, six different A Cats won races.

Three more boats have graced the waters of Barnegat Bay since 2001. *Torch* was commissioned by Peter Kellogg, built once again by John Brady to Sweisguth's design. She sailed very nicely in her debut season, as did *Witch*, built by Bill de Rouville in Lanoka Harbor for Austin and Gwen Fragomen. And Steve Brick, owner of *Lotus*, one of the older boats in the fleet, commissioned Beaton's to build *Lightning*, which was launched in 2003. In 2005, Brick had *Lotus* restored to proper weight.

This crew of Bat *looks stunned to have won the Wanamaker Trophy.*

To sail an A Cat well takes at least seven crew to gain enough stability, although the early BBYRA limited the class to only six. Ballast is important. In the future a maximum crew weight might be considered. The helmsman has to have enough strength and endurance to hang on to the tiller, and the main sheet trimmer has to have enough brute power to haul on the line without benefit of winches. The tactician has to be aware of the idiosyncrasies of the various boats. Some sail fast upwind, some fly before the wind. The rest of the crew must be content to lie flat on the decks. And, of course, bail out the water. When an A Cat tacks, the crew scrambles around the front of the mast to avoid the boom. Jibing in a breeze is a challenge. Centerboards have to be hauled up in shallow water, as the bay has a sticky, muddy bottom.

When they first appeared, A Cats captivated the attention of sailors and non-sailors alike. It is no different today. Millie Applegate was succinct in her thoughts, "Once you get on an A Cat, you never want to get off." The same names keep coming up as crew. A Cat trophies seem to pass regularly back and forth between all the boats, one of the great attractions of the class. The competition is fierce and the races hotly contested. The class as a whole tends to self-regulate and that continues to attract dedicated owners.

A Cat owners are motivated people. Maintaining one of them is a big commitment. Nelson Hartranft led the way and Peter Kellogg continues to carry the torch, investing in the continuation of the class and allowing sailors with the requisite dedication access to these intoxicating sailboats.

THE BOATS

Painting by John English.

Mary Ann | *Bat* | *Helen* | *Forcem* | *Tamwock*

Spy | *Lotus* | *Wasp* | *Tamwock II*

Ghost | *Vapor* | *Raven* | *Spy II* | *Torch* | *Witch* | *Lightning*

Bob Adams stands up at the helm to get a clear view of the racecourse.

Mary Ann | *Built in: 1922* | *Built for: Charles McKeehan* | *Named for: Charlie McKeehan's mother* | *Current Owners: Bob and Tay Adams*
Sail numbers: MA, M9 | *Designer: Charles D. Mower* | *Builder: Morton Johnson, Bay Head, New Jersey*
Restored by Benjamin River Marine in Brooklin, Maine, 1985

MARY ANN

Mr. Charles McKeehan built *Mary Ann* in 1922 to race for the Toms River Yacht Club Challenge Cup. She was the first A Cat built and is the only A Cat still sailing with its original sail number. *Mary Ann* is a Charles Mower design built by Morton Johnson in Bay Head. It was restored in 1985 by Benjamin River Marine in Brooklin, Maine.

Bob Adams, *current owner of* Mary Ann

These boats almost sail like dinghies. And yet they are so much larger. But they feel like a dinghy to me. They don't belong out in the bay when it is blowing 25 knots, being torn up. You have a lot of money at stake in these boats and if they ever have a collision with one another, God help us.

People in the class really prefer to sail shorter races and more of them. It was my suggestion to Roy (Wilkins) that we go to double races on certain BBYRA weekends. The older boats have a better shot, and the races are much more interesting if the courses are shorter. I don't know anybody who races A Cats who doesn't enjoy the mini regattas that are held down on Toms River or the Callahan Regatta up on Metedeconk River. I think everybody likes the Beaton Cup.

Bob O'Brien, *former commodore of Bay Head Yacht Club*

Two people in particular can be congratulated for saving the fleet. Nelson Hartranft, who owned every boat in the late '60s and '70s. He fixed them up one by one, to the extent that he was able, and kept them sailing. And then along came Peter Kellogg. He

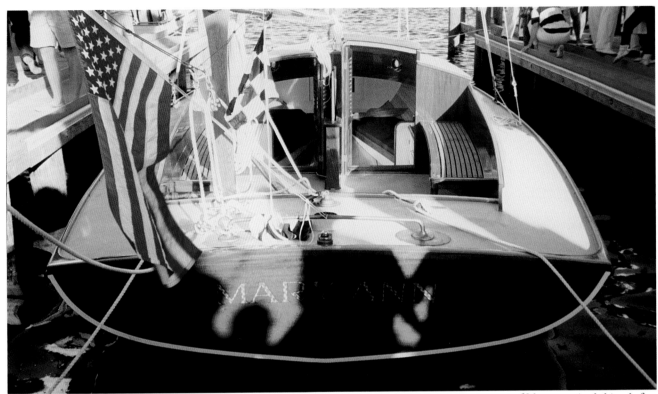

Ironically, I think we probably never had as much fun on the boat after it was rebuilt, because it was sort of like a survival thing before it was rebuilt. There were times when you could see daylight through the topside seams and water would be pouring in.

—John Hale, former owner of *Mary Ann*

picked up where Nelson left off. Not only did he improve the boats, back in 1985 he was responsible for sending the *Mary Ann* up to the Benjamin River in Maine where she was virtually rebuilt. The guy told me maybe one plank remains from 1922 but everything else is new. She is still out there competing after all these years.

Charlie Lord, current owner of Bat

My uncle, Woodgy Law, had the *Mary Ann* in the '60s and '70s. Woodgy crewed for my dad on *Lotus* for a year or two and then when Woodgy bought the *Mary Ann*, my dad crewed for him. Woodgy allowed juniors to come onboard, and he allowed you to lay up on the foredeck. That's when they used to lay down on the sides, and hold on to the shrouds. I was fortunate enough to do that a number of times. I fell in love with the boats. I always loved the A Cats and I always said I wanted to own one when I grew up.

Gale Yetman, current owner of Spy

I was late for a race so I ran down the Nelson Marina to get on *Mary Ann* to go off to the Island Heights race. My daughter, Coury, who was nine months old, was in her car seat. I grabbed the seat with her in it and put her down below. The boat leaks so much that there was always someone down below to watch her. She must be the youngest person ever to race on an A Cat. The only time I was nervous was when we were on a reach and it was windy. The waves were coming over the bow and she was taking on water. When the crew said, "hey, what about the baby," Richard and John eased up and stopped the water from coming in. My daughter is grown up and sailing out in California so I guess it was a positive experience for her.

Casey Yetman aboard Mary Ann *(1979).*

John Hale

It was kind of interesting how we ended up buying the boat in 1982. *Mary Ann* belonged to Richard Yetman and John Engle at the time. Richard was an invited guest to my wedding reception at the Toms River Yacht Club. I guess we all were in a pretty relaxed frame of mind near the end of the reception. Somehow Richard offered to sell me the boat, and I ended up making a deal with Marshall Warner to buy it, unbeknownst to my brand new bride at the time.

It was in pretty tired condition at that point. There were only a couple of boats that were actually still sailing. Nelson Hartranft had launched the

Center left in red, grandson of Ed Schoettle, original owner of Forcem, *onboard* Mary Ann. *Bob Adams, in the stripped shirt, is at the helm. Tay Adams is to the left of Bob with the white hat. Lifejackets were mandatory on this breezy day.*

Wasp one or two years prior to our acquiring *Mary Ann*. *Bat* was just about to go down for the count. *Spy* was on the water and that was it to the best of my recollection. There wasn't a lot of parity in terms of the condition of the boats. And occasionally I guess Nelson would feel magnanimous and actually give us handicap advantages. Roy Wilkins, on the other hand, after he finished rebuilding the *Spy*, refused to give anybody any consideration for differences of condition on the boats.

I remember we were sailing to the last race of our first season with the boat, and we were about halfway there and our rudder fell off. This was the state that boat was in.

Mary Ann *crosses* Spy. *The sails look like shark fins. Notice both helmsmen pulling hard on the tillers.*

The Mary Ann *goes very well when it is reefed. I used to joke that it even went better when it's reefed.*   —Bob Adams

After the second season, the boat was in such bad condition that if the pumps failed when the boat was in its slip, it would sink in about 12 minutes. So we knew we had to do something. I decided to undertake a massive refit, not knowing that much about boats at all, and I actually recaulked every single seam in the boat. There was a fair amount of pressure because there weren't that many boats and everybody felt that we had an obligation to get the boat in the water in time for the season.

After the refit, the boat actually was tight, and it stayed tight for about the first two to three races. But then the boat started to open up again. The old mast step on those boats was set up in a

MARY ANN OWNERS	
Charles McKeehan	1922–1925
Ed Brooks	1926–1929
Harry Gale	1930–1935
G.E. Robertson	1936–1940
Harry Newman	1941–1944
Harry Gale	1944–1953
Ed Wogen	1954–1957
Bob Byrns	1958–1961
Karl Bock	1961–1964
Warren Law	1962–1973
John Amon	1974–1975
Nelson Hartranft	1978–1979
John Engle/Richard Yetman	1980–1982
Marshall Warner/John Hale	1983–1988
Toms River Seaport Society	1989–1998
Bob and Tay Adams	1999–2005

The racing barrel at Good Luck Point is known today as "E." Years ago it was barrel 5 and was part of the Wanamaker course configuration. During a race on that course Millie Applegate was part of the foredeck crew laying decks on Mary Ann, while her husband, Brit Applegate, was at the helm of Mary Ann that day. When rounding barrel 5, Millie ended up in the water. The reasons for what happened next are unclear. Whether it was to maintain the leading position or to continue the pursuit of the leaders is unknown, but Millie was left to tread water. Luckily Millie was a good swimmer because she stayed afloat at the barrel until Mary Ann rounded barrel 5 again. Mary Ann finished that race with a full crew, Millie included. There was never a lengthy discussion of the incident when both of my parents were present. Perhaps it was better that way.

—Mike Frankovich, former owner of Bat

Start off Island Heights Yacht Club (circa 1925).

way that it just made the boat twist. There wasn't enough support forward so you'd get under load and all of a sudden the seams would start to open up and the water would start to gush in.

Then Roy Wilkins offered us an interesting proposition. He knew a philanthropist who had expressed an interest in supporting the fleet, and would we be interested in a traditional repair process? The boat missed two sailing seasons, possibly three. It was completely rebuilt from the keel all the way up by a boatyard up in Brooklin, Maine. And, of course, after we relaunched it, the transom floated high and dry out of the water and it was really as if it was brand new again.

Woogie Law, former owner of Mary Ann

Ann Hatridge was one of the few women to crew on A Cats. In a 1977 race she crewed with me on *Mary Ann* and insisted on sitting on the boom going downwind. We were leading the race when the gooseneck broke with Ann on the boom. She fell, bounced off the cabin, and landed in the water. *Spy* was directly behind us and scooped up Ann. After the race, which we won, *Spy* wanted to protest *Mary Ann* for finishing without the number of crew that started the race. I responded that I was going to protest *Spy* for finishing the race with more crew than they started with. Everyone laughed and *Mary Ann* took the race without any protests.

Four years ago, down in Little Egg, I was crewing on Ghost *and we were leading the race beating to the finish upwind. And Chris Chadwick on the* Mary Ann *with George Schuld and Brent Wagner on his crew—this is a gold-plated A Cat group—was second and he instituted a tacking duel against us and he won the race. So with a good skipper and crew, the* Mary Ann *is competitive and we have seen it to be so. It is really a very good boat.*

—Bob O'Brien

Bat | *Built in: 1923* | *Built for: Ed Crabbe* | *Current Owner: Charlie Lord* | *Designer: Charles D. Mower* | *Builder: Morton Johnson, Bay Head, New Jersey* | *Sail numbers: T1, S6, I93, IH1, L1* | *Restored in 1986 by Robert Lostrom, Island Heights, New Jersey*

BAT

Charlie Lord

My grandfather, Fred Winkelman, bought the *Lotus* back in about '52, I believe from Ed Schoettle. I have some great pictures hanging on my walls. Around 1959 he passed it off to my dad, Russ Lord. My grandfather and my dad enjoyed some championships on the bay and we have some great memories. They didn't allow us to go racing, obviously, but they'd take us out for a sail once in a while. I grew up with the *Bat*, *Mary Ann*, *Lotus*, and the *Spy*.

I just think they are the most beautiful boats in the world. When I look at pictures of the *Bat*, or any of them, it almost takes my breath away. I don't know how to explain it. I love that design. The hull, just the layout of the boat. They are just absolutely gorgeous to me. They're a lot of power, a lot of boat. There is nothing like when the wind is blowing and the boat is up on its side. You're holding on to the tiller, that big boat tiller, and it's bent like a J, and you are holding on for dear life. It is taking all the strength you have just to keep the boat going the way you want it to. It is exciting. You need a fairly steady crew, at least five people that sail with you every weekend. If you have different people, they don't know what to do and any one could get in trouble in a heartbeat. We've got a good crew that we're happy with now, and they love it, and they're always there.

My wife and I bought the *Bat* intending to sail with our families. One of the things that is really special to us is the camaraderie between all the owners and the crew, from people who have sailed on them in the past to people who sail on them presently.

We always wondered where the name Bat *came from. I had heard a lot of different stories, and probably the one that is most accurate, but we really don't know, is when they built it that somebody up there at Johnson's said well, this boat is going to go like a Bat out of hell. That makes it more appropriate than some of the other stories.* —Alicemay Weber-Wright

The first time I can ever remember being on a sailboat was on the Bat. *I think I was three years old and we were off Windy Cove, sailing along in a gentle breeze, in the evening or late afternoon. Every time a little gust would come along, the boat would heel a little bit, and I was scared to death. I remember crying because I didn't want the boat to heel at that age. It's funny what a long way I've come* —Dan Crabbe

Fortunately, there were people that had the same love that we do of bringing them back and restoring them to the beauties they once were. My grandfather, when he bought the *Lotus*, had it totally restored before he ever sailed it. That's probably what made him so competitive. His boat was in better shape than everybody else's. It takes people that really love them and are committed to doing that type of thing. That is why I try to get the juniors on board. If you get them out there now, then 20 years from now they're going to want to get an A Cat. It is a nice thing to have one at your club. When we bought the *Bat*, there were some senior people, my mom was in her seventies, that were standing on the end of the Lavallette Yacht Club dock. They were clapping when we towed it home.

Dan Crabbe, grandson of Ed Crabbe, the original owner of **Bat**

I first raced when I was 10. I would race a Comet in the morning, and I was sometimes asked to crew on the A Cat in the afternoon. I was always told to get in the guest position—really to keep me out of the way, because the guest position of the A Cat was right up in the bow, half over the rail, lying down flat so there wasn't any wind resistance.

The waves, especially in heavy air, would just come in and you would get soaking wet. Then when you were going downwind on the run, you'd come aft. My job was to go below, bail what water was in the bilge, and then open beer cans for the crew.

I remember a story about my father.

Usually after the race they'd come in on a southerly wind and they'd have to come in toward the boathouse then round up into the wind, drop the sail, drift back, then pick up a mooring.

One time my grandfather, in tie and jacket, along with some of his friends were down there watching the *Bat* come in. And my father, I guess was maybe trying to show off, although he didn't say that, but as they rounded up, someone forgot to let the backstay go and the boat didn't round up—it's blowing about

Alicemay Weber-Wright steers Bat.

My stepfather Bob Schneider raced the Bat *with the Crabbes. I was taken on the boat to get me out of the house as much as anything. My job was to lay on the deck and pump. There was always a lot of pumping back in those days with A Cats. I can tell you there wasn't a lot of conversation as there is nowadays on the boat. I was brought up that way. You don't have conversations when you are racing. If you're not telling the captain or somebody about other boats or the wind, then you don't say anything. You don't talk about what you did last night or are going to do next week for sure.*

—Alicemay Weber-Wright

15 knots out of the south and the boat slammed into the concrete bulkhead. The backstay is broken, and the mast just fell down, broke right at the deck, and fell across the lawn.

My grandfather just looked at it. He motioned to his friends, they got back in their Model T Ford and just drove off. That was one bad experience.

But when my father tells it, he does so in a funny way.

Buzz Reynolds, son of Jim Reynolds, former owner of Spy

The A Cat class was dying in the early '70s when John Peets, Allan Terhune, and John Engle of Island Heights bought the *Bat* for $2,500 and fixed her up enough to be able to sail. As teenagers, they used the *Bat* as their personal party boat, going out every night with friends and sailing until the late hours.

One night John Peets walked out to the end of the boom and was sitting there drinking his beer. We were passing Long Point marker when a puff of wind lifted up the boom and the main sheet caught around the marker. I still clearly see John hanging on to Long Point for dear life, with the *Bat* jibing around in circles.

While a dangerous situation because of the darkness, the wind, and the threat of losing the mast, we were all laughing so hard—John kept yelling that he couldn't hang on because the marker was full of seagull sh!!!. I don't know how we ever we rescued John and the *Bat*, but everything ended up OK. We still re-tell the story with sincere laughter.

Mike Frankovich

I think Roy Wilkins was really the first one to get

Charlie talked about A Cats all through our courtship, and buying an A Cat became a dream of both of ours. I love it because it is such a great family thing. —Laurie Lord, current owner of *Bat*

me involved when they restored *Spy*. I was still in college at that point or I had just gotten out. Way back when I was 10 or 11, I had the opportunity to sail with Brit and Millie Applegate on the *Lotus*. I really thought what an overpowering vessel these things were. But the A Cats, when we were growing up, were the boats that always sank. Then Roy restored his and he made it look pristine. I thought

Anytime you get somebody who has never sailed on an A Cat but is a sailor, it is always kind of neat to see their expression when you tack or jibe the boat and they have to walk forward around the mast. They just can't fathom that. Once they do it the first time, they understand the Chinese fire drill that takes place, especially in heavy air.

—Cory Wingerter, owner of *Raven*

it was a great idea: if you restore a whole fleet of these, and they don't sink, and they all look pristine, this is going to be really something.

Then I got out of school and was looking to put together a syndicate because I couldn't afford to restore an A Cat on my own. I came across this guy, Bob Lostrom, who was interested in redoing an A Cat. I said I had one in mind and I told him about the *Bat*. So I take Bob up to Beaton's to show him what we are buying. You could see through the bottom down to the ground and the weeds were coming through.

BAT TROPHIES

Bay Championship
1931, 1932, 1934, 1937, 1938, 1939, 1940, 1946, 1947, 1948, 1949, 1951, 1972, 1973, 1975, 1978, 1980, 1986, 1987, 1991

Middleton Cup
1927, 1928, 1941, 1948, 1949, 1951, 1962, 1972, 1973, 1975, 1978, 1980, 1986, 1987, 1991

Sewell Cup
1932, 1934, 1937, 1939, 1949, 1946, 1947, 1948, 1949, 1961, 1963, 1970, 1972, 1973, 1974, 1975, 1978, 1979, 1980, 1986, 1987

Morgan Cup
1924, 1931, 1932, 1934, 1937, 1938, 1939, 1940, 1946, 1947, 1948, 1949, 1951, 1972, 1973, 1976, 1978, 1980, 1981, 1983, 1989, 1990, 1991

Challenge Cup
1925, 1929, 1931, 1932, 1933, 1939, 1948, 1949, 1953, 1954, 1962, 1972, 1973, 1978, 1980, 1987, 1993

Barry Connolly was on the bow line and started talking to a dockside female at the Mantoloking Yacht Club. Somehow he forgot to secure the bow line. The boat fell back and the mainsheet fowled a piling and drew in tight and the Bat tipped over. No one was hurt and there was no damage to any of the boats at the dock or the Bat. Dave Beaton showed up with a motorized pump and we were back up and sailing that afternoon. There is a picture that shows the boat going over with the centerboard out of the water and a lone head (Jack Boyer) peering over the rail as the boat goes over.

—Neil Prothers, former owner of *Bat*

The key to sailing an A Cat efficiently is smooth coordination between the helmsman and the mainsail trimmer.

Simultaneous to this event, Steve Brick bought the *Lotus*, and since Beaton was busy refurbishing the *Lotus* we were going to have to wait a year and a half. So Bob goes, "I'll fix the boat. We're going to take it to my shop and we're going to fiberglass it." We did 85 percent of the work ourselves.

And there are some funny stories.

I was in charge of painting the deck of the A Cat after we rebuilt it. I think that was on a Saturday and we were bringing the boat back midweek, on a Wednesday—and the paint on the deck is still wet. We're thinking, "Wow this paint is still wet." Now I'm reading the directions to the paint. Turns out, you were supposed to put hardener in it. So the first race that we sailed, the one where the boom broke, everybody got green butts.

We ended up scraping off all the paint after that race. We had to take it all off. We just basically sailed it with the fiberglass showing through.

Arleen Lostrom, wife of former owner of **Bat**

The first time that I went on the *Bat* was for an evening sail up the Toms River with Bob Lostrom, who I was just beginning to date. We were getting to know each other and Bob was not looking where he was going. As we sailed by the Island Heights Yacht Club dock our long boom hit the flag mast on the end of the dock and broke it in two. Then we sailed to Long Point and kept running aground. I thought this guy was an accomplished sailor! On the way back Bob was not paying attention and the *Bat* hit and broke two channel markers outside of Nelson's Marina. It was quite the first A Cat ride. That year when Bob got the seamanship award from Island Heights Yacht Club, as a joke they gave him part of the flag mast he had broken in two. We had great times on the *Bat*.

BAT OWNERS	
Ed Crabbe	*1923–1952*
Dick Irons	*1953–1957*
Ernie Hangartner	*1958–1959*
Neil Prothers, Bill Wilson,	
Jack Boyer, Barry Connolly	*1960–1973*
Butch Haddon/Allen Terhune	*1974–1975*
John Peets, Bob Schmicker,	
John Engle	*1974–1976*
Charles Cox	*1975–1976*
Nelson Hartranft III	*1976–1984*
Mike Frankovich/Robert Lostrom	*1984–1999*
Charlie Lord	*2000–2005*

Nelson Hartranft III, third from the right, circa 1979.

Neil and I were married in 1963 and all the spouses, girlfriends, or whatever were part of the crew. I think one of the highlights of the summer for me was going to the Eno's race, which was a race from anchor. And then we all had dinner at Captain's Inn. That was a social thing. We sailed back, and pretty much that was a very, very long day—and into the next day—before you got back up bay.

—Ellen Prothers, wife of former owner of *Bat*

HELEN

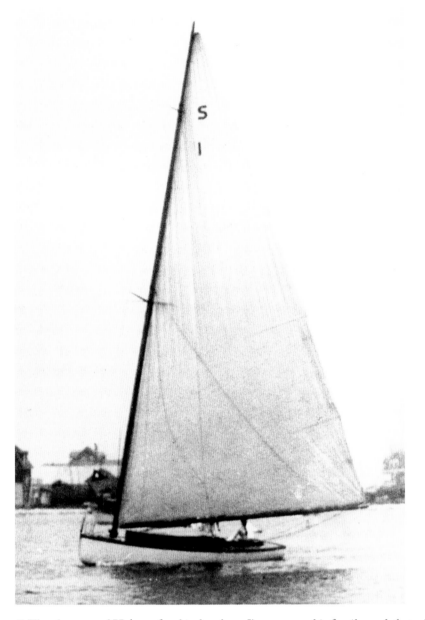

"Buoy Room" Thatcher named Helen *after his daughter. I'm not sure his family used that nickname, but it was a good one.*   —Peter Kellogg

Forcem *and* Helen *were built to beat* Mary Ann. *Both boats were reportedly slow and only raced one year. After two years* Helen *went down bay and her fate is unknown. Frank Thatcher went on to build* Spy *in 1924, the sister ship to* Mary Ann.   —Roy Wilkins, owner of *Spy*

Helen | *Built in: 1923 (only raced 1 year) | Built for: Frank Thatcher | Named for: Frank Thatcher's daughter*
Designer: Charles D. Mower | Builder: Hoppers Basin | Sail number: S1

FORCEM

Rumor has it the Schoettles scuttled Forcem *in the Toms River just below their house.*

Forcem | *Built in: 1923 (only raced 1 year)* | *Built for: Edwin J. Schoettle and Ed Harrington* | *Named for: Four partners*
Designer: Francis Sweisguth | *Builder: John Kirk, Toms River, New Jersey* | *Sail number: 4 SM*

Tamwock (sail #8) during prestart maneuvers, circa 1924.

Tamwock | *Built in: 1923* | *Built for: Francis Larkin* | *Named for: a fish* | *Designer: Francis Sweisguth*
Builder: John Kirk, Toms River, New Jersey | *Sail numbers: S1, IH8, 8* | *Destroyed by fire in 1940*

TAMWOCK

Mike Frankovich

Snapper's parents were really kind of like the pioneers of the A Cat fleet. Brit was born in 1893. He was the first so-called hired gun of the A Cat fleet. As the story goes, Schoettle hired him to be his chauffer for the summer and steer the boat. That is when the original *Tamwock* was out. They were kicking tail and taking no prisoners. When Brit sailed the *Tamwock*, there came a point when the BBYRA said you have to be affiliated with a yacht club to sail. There was a by-law in the Island Heights Yacht Club that said that if you lived in town year-round you couldn't belong to the yacht club. And that rule was really designed to keep the locals out.

They have repealed it now. But when the yacht club was originally founded, I guess the people that lived there year-round were like hunters and farmers and clammers, you know that gang. And the yacht club didn't want to associate with any of them, so they put this in their by-laws. But they must have just taken it out prior to Brit wanting to join.

And Snapper doesn't know who the fellows were who sponsored Brit. I know Schoettle was one, but a bunch of them did. And the Board of Governors wasn't going to approve his application so all the sponsors had to threaten to quit. They were all going to just resign. But when they threatened to quit, the Board of Governors approved and got Brit in.

TAMWOCK OWNERS

Francis Larkin	*1923–1926*
H. H. Cross	*1927–1932*
Russ Perkins	*1933*
Albert Diss	*1934–1940*

TAMWOCK TROPHIES

Bay Championship
1926, 1928, 1929, 1930, 1936

Middleton Cup
1925, 1926, 1936, 1938

Sewell Cup
1926, 1928, 1930, 1931, 1938

Morgan Cup
1928, 1929, 1930, 1936

Challenge Cup
1928

The old Spy team from the bow back: Alyssa Wilkins, Jane Wilkins, Maggie Groff, Onie Bolduck, Jim Reynolds, Roy Wilkins, Gary Stewart, Chris Chadwick.

Spy | Built in: 1924 | Built for: Frank Thatcher | Named for: Seaside Park Yacht | Current owner: Toms River Seaport Museum
Designer: Charles D. Mower | Builder: Morton Johnson, Bay Head, New Jersey | Sail numbers: S11, S1, IH 78, SPY, IH SPY
Rebuilt in 1984 at Beaton's Boatyard, West Mantoloking, New Jersey

SPY

Nelson Hartranft, saved **Spy** *in 1975*

What was on my mind? To save the class. When I was a kid in Ocean Gate I started crewing for a guy on a sneakbox. He was a couple of years older than me. We would always marvel at the A Cats. The *Bat*, in those days, was moored off Ocean Gate, raced by a dentist from the Philadelphia area. It was quite a thing for 12-year-old kids to see these A Cats racing.

I just fell in love with them at that point in my life. When I saw that they were going downhill in disrepair I just decided that I would try to do something about it.

The *Spy* was owned by a fellow named Jim McKay from Ocean Gate. That's the one that I started out with. I bought the *Spy* in 1975, and we won the Bay Championship in 1976 with it. My wife and a buddy of mine's wife spent most of their time down in the cabin with a hand pump, the old-fashioned galvanized hand pump. Pumping water into the centerboard well so that we could continue to float. The ladies never saw the light of day as far as racing is concerned until the race was over. But that's how it all got started.

Then after the *Spy*, I bought the *Bat* from a group of fellows from over in the Island Heights area, and my son raced the boat for a few years. We got that in decent shape.

And then some guys from Ocean Gate had the *Mary Ann* and they blew out the stem heading down the Forked River—that was when we used to race down the bay for the Ocean Gate Race, down the Forked River for dinner either at the Forked River House or the Captain's Inn. So a friend of mine, Karl Bock, he is a past commodore of the

When Nelson Hartranft saw Lotus stuck in the ice, he was inspired to restore her.

The Wilkins family enjoys one last sail on Spy before it retires to the Toms River Seaport Museum.

SPY OWNERS

Frank Thatcher	1924–1930
Fernand Schoettle	1931–1934
Earl & Ed Van Sciver	1935–1945
Larry & Dick Power	1946–1948
G.C. Clark	1949
Wayne Barr	1950–1955
Don & Bob Sayia	1956–1971
Jim McKay	1972–1974
Nelson Hartranft	1975–1977
Roy Wilkins/Charlie Cox	1978–1980
Roy Wilkins, Jane Wilkins,	
Jim Reynolds, Maggie Groff,	
Richard Groff, Gary Stewart,	
Christel Stewart, Fran Brady	1981–2000
Toms River Seaport Museum	2001–2005

Barnegat Bay Yacht Racing Association, and I took it up to Beaton's and we fixed the stem up there.

The *Lotus* used to race for the Toms River Seaport Society, that was after the Applegate family sold it to the Seaport Society. What they did was they left it up there in the Toms River at the Seaport Society under full rig all winter long, sitting in the ice. Half-frozen and half-sunk in the ice.

I said, "You guys get that thing up to Beaton's without destroying the keel and the centerboard and what have you"—it was sitting on the bottom and I was afraid they were just going to twist it and turn it and rip the bottom out—and I said, "I'll buy it." That's what they did. So that's how I wound up owning all four of the boats.

I sold each one of them with the stipulation and understanding that they would all be kept in as good

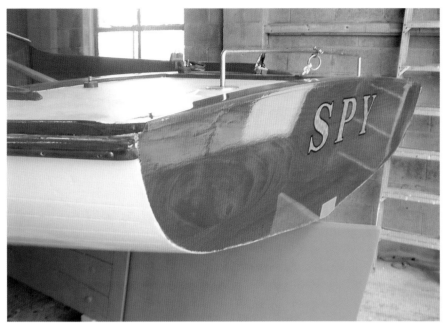

Spy in her final port after a complete restoration at the Toms River Seaport Society in the Hawkins Building.

Racing wasn't the primary reason to buy the boat.

We sailed *Spy* as soon as we bought her in September, every day, every Friday night. All through the '80s we'd just sail up and down the river with friends, go to the Anchor Inn for dinner, and then sail until midnight, singing and stuff. The racing was fun, even though there were only three or four boats. But it was a great, great boat to be out with your friends on.

My children grew up on *Spy*. They sailed it. They raced it. They just had a great time on it. It's like part of the family.

Right before we fixed *Spy*, we were sailing in the Forked River race, sailing down bay, and Jane, who never saw daylight for the four years before we fixed her because she was always down pumping, yelled, "I can see the bay! I can see the bay through the bottom of the boat!" The mast was going through the bottom of the boat. The keel had broken. It was hinged and the pressure of the mast was opening the boat up, and I could see the aqua green of the water—a big gusher coming through. That was pretty wild. I thought the whole boat was going to break in half. We headed for shore and just beached her, then we towed the boat to Beaton's from that beach.

shape as possible and that they would be raced. If whoever bought them decided that they didn't want to do it anymore, I would buy them back.

I had no idea that the class would be like it is today. It is an absolutely miraculous thing.

Roy Wilkins, owner of Spy

Friends of mine—Butch Haddon and John Engle—bought the *Bat* in the mid '70s. My wife and I went out sailing with them and it was a very social, fun thing to do. And then *Spy* became available in 1978. A good friend of mine, Charlie Cox, and I decided it would be great to bring *Spy* back to life.

At the time I was an adaptive physical education teacher in Toms River and the boat was a great platform to take my students out sailing. And I wanted to take my family and friends out sailing.

Jane Wilkins at Beaton's with Spy *during rebuild.*

Our daughter Alyssa got married on the Spy. *I dug a hole in the bottom for the rudder to allow the boat close enough to the beach and we pulled* Spy *up to a dock. We took the boom off. Jane decorated the mast. Everybody had chairs right on the beach. They got married on the boat and then we all went to the yacht club and partied all night.* —Roy Wilkins

Maggie Groff, Jane Wilkins, Bob Lostrom, Roy Wilkins, Chris Chadwick, Gary Stewart, and Jim Reynolds winning the Sewell Cup and the Bay Championship.

It's pretty frightening. Especially because it's a historic boat and so many things race through your mind when you see the keel broken. It's like being in a car wreck. You look at it and you think it's totaled. What do you do? You have that to deal with, plus the safety of the people on the boat. We were way down bay so there weren't a lot of support boats around.

Maggie Groff, owner of Spy

I've been a partner with *Spy* since '82 or '83. I had sailed on the *Bat* years before that when I was in college. From that experience I was enthralled and intrigued by the A Cats, and that is the reason we got involved in *Spy*. I'm a real sucker for tradition. You know, it is just that these boats have been around for so long, such classics, wooden, so gorgeous. Our boat always has a lot of women on it. We've got more partners than many boats too, four couples as partners in our boat. Each summer we sort of divvy up our responsibilities, and they vary.

Roy Wilkins and his grandsons enjoy the dedication of Spy.

Fran Brady, *owner of* Spy

We were up bay and it was extremely windy. Along with Alyssa Wilkins, Jane Wilkins, Gary Stewart, Helene McMullan, Billy de Rouville, Roy, and myself, we had a junior sailor named Reed Johnson, who was nine at the time. Roy put Reed down below and had him pump as well as move the electric pumps. At one point we were jibing and Billy de Rouville couldn't unlock the leeward backstay. We were going over after the jibe, with Billy now underwater unlocking the backstay. Just as he unlocked it underwater Roy reached down and with superhuman strength pulled Billy into the cockpit. I couldn't believe it. Reed's eyes were the size of saucers. Then on the next leg it happened again and this time Alyssa was underwater. Once again Roy grabbed her and yanked her back into the cockpit. It was the most amazing day I ever had on an A Cat. I am sure Reed, Alyssa, and Billy will never forget that race.

I've wanted to sail one of these things ever since I was a little kid. You'd go out to the BBYRA races, and you'd see a couple of them limping around. They were just the most amazing things I'd ever seen. I remember telling my mom that someday I'm going to sail one, and I think she thought I was insane because there were only two or three left. But the opportunity presented itself and I got involved with Roy Wilkins. He inspired all this. —Gary Stewart

Gary Stewart

I was racing Lasers and E Scows like everybody else in their twenties, and just out of the U.S. Merchant Marine Academy. One Friday night at the Toms River Yacht Club Roy asked me to sail on *Spy* the next day. I had never sailed on an A Cat before. I went out there with him and Jim Reynolds, it was an honor to be there.

Roy told me, "it is as easy as this: if it blows we're going to win. If it is light air, well, that will kill us." Well, it was light air. I said to Roy, "we're just going to cover *Bat* everywhere they go and match race them," and looked at the race that way. We got to the leeward mark and we were side by side, and we ended up beating them. I don't think Roy had ever really sailed an A Cat that aggressively before. The rest was kind of history. We just sailed more and more together.

I had just gotten out of law school when Roy and Maggie offered me a partnership in the boat for a very modest sum. I was moving five hours away, and I really thought that over time the glory of it and the dream of it would just kind of fade. But I found just the opposite happened. Some new boats were put into the fleet and it's gotten to be more competitive and more fun. I just really live to do it.

*Even with the broken spar, * Spy *finds a way to fly their battle flag.*

Terrifying experiences on these boats happen pretty much anytime the wind gets above 20 and you have to jibe. I remember one time at Seaside we were going upwind and, right before we got to the A barrel right off the club, all of a sudden there was a pop and the tiller hit me literally in the chest. The stay had let go and the mast just came down over the water. Breaking a mast on an A Cat is something I would never want to have to go through again.
—Gary Stewart

Spy *and* Mary Ann *battle for the Bay Championship. John Engle, in the white shirt (left), is standing. Charlie Cox is in the red shirt (right), with Butch Haddon in the stripped shirt trimming mainsail.*

It has always been tradition in the class to avoid any type of collision because the boats were so old and delicate. The last Bay race in 1977, Roy and Charlie Cox owned the Spy *and asked me to be tactician. Terry Kempton was on board Nelson Hartranft's boat and Peter Commette was on another boat. Peter, Terry, and I had grown up racing against each other and were intense competitors. The fleet was four boats total. Everyone was keen to win the last race of the BBYRA and the beautiful bowl that goes with it. The wind was southeast and building to 15 knots.* Spy *won the start and led around the first mark, C barrel in front of SPYC, with the crowd cheering. From there it was downwind to F barrel, off the Seaside bridge.* Spy *was slow on a run and got overlapped on the inside by all three boats. Literally, all four A Cats were overlapped going into F barrel. As outside boat, I told Charlie, who was steering, to take it wide, let the other three pass, then slip inside at the mark. Charlie did as I said, but as we turned to head up and pass inside, Terry Kempton, helmsman on the boat in front of us, turned around, smiled, and said "Buzzy—no room, don't try it" and headed up to close the hole we were going for. Charlie realized there was no room, tried to head down, but our forestay caught Terry's boom, snagged on their outhaul cleat, and we dragged him into hitting the other rounding boats. All four A Cats were banging into each other, everyone yelling and screaming. It was my fault and I earned the name "Crash" Reynolds that day. It marked the beginning of the intensity brought to the class to win, sometimes with not such great results, but always with great stories to tell. That is what keeps the class alive, the ability to have 6–10 people sail together in a relatively simple boat with tremendous power, and then to swap stories afterwards in a friendly social atmosphere.*

—Buzz Reynolds

Lotus | *Built in: 1925* | *Built for: Bob Truitt* | *Current owner: Steve Brick* | *Designer: Charles D. Mower*
Builder: Morton Johnson, Bay Head, New Jersey | *Sail numbers: IH-L, ib11, LO, 4sm*
Restored in 1986 and 2005 by Beaton's Boatyard, West Mantoloking, New Jersey

LOTUS

Steve Brick, current owner of Lotus

One of the most incredible things about the A Cat fleet is the number of people who have sailed on one. People you wouldn't expect. Sometimes I'll bring up the A Cat in conversation just to see how well-known they are, and a tremendous number of people are aware of the A Cats on Barnegat Bay: non-sailors, people not necessarily from the local area. On any given Saturday, there are a hundred or so people participating in the BBYRA on A Cats.

Roy Wilkins and I are boyhood friends from Island Heights. I crewed for Roy on the *Spy* in the early '80s. I decided I wanted to get back into competitive sailing, and I have one brother who sails an Ensign on the bay, and one brother who sails an E Scow. I didn't necessarily want to be in their fleets, so that left A Cats. Plus, we felt A Cats were a perfect boat for both racing on Saturdays and daysailing on the bay other times. And there is the history of the class.

At the time, there were three A Cats out of commission and Nelson Hartranft had bought them. They were in Beaton's just sitting on blocks with weeds growing through their floor boards. I paid $1,000 for what was left of the *Lotus*.

I had a choice of Bat *or* Lotus. *And through no particular logic, I selected* Lotus.
　　　　　　　　　　　　　　　　　—Steve Brick

LOTUS TROPHIES

Bay Championship
1953, 1954, 1955, 1956, 1957, 1958, 1969, 1971, 1977

Middleton Cup
1929, 1930, 1931, 1937, 1940, 1953, 1954, 1955, 1957, 1958, 1959, 1961, 1969, 1971, 1977

Sewell Cup
1925, 1936, 1941, 1951, 1953, 1954, 1955, 1957, 1958, 1977

Morgan Cup
1953, 1954, 1955, 1956, 1957, 1958, 1969, 1971

Challenge Cup
1930, 1934, 1935, 1936, 1937, 1940, 1955, 1956, 1957, 1958, 1968, 1969

Tommy Beaton inspects the hull with the assistance of Adam Brick.

Snapper Applegate

Yes, we did own the *Lotus*. It was right around the time the A Cats were down to four. I think there was only one sailing in 1972. One sail-able. Then *Spy* was dragged out of the bushes by Jim McKay and my father crewed on that. That was the year that *Spy* won the Toms River Cup. My dad was on board. I was just looking over some old newspaper articles: the headline in the paper was "Applegate Shows the Way." It was pretty interesting. He was asked whether or not he was the navigator and he said, "Nope." And they asked him whether or not he was the tactician and he said, "Nope." They said how did you help these guys? He said, "I just told them where to go." That's both, navigator and tactician. But that was his comment. That was my dad.

Lotus, *Schoettle period, 1931. The crew looks very relaxed. I like the Island Heights burgee flying from the forestay.*

Lotus, *1995.*

None of the crew seem to want to get off the rail.

The most horrifying moment I recall is when Peter Kellogg sailed majestically into the Mantoloking Yacht Club in about 1966. He then owned the Lotus, *and he had just won the Beck Crabbe trophy. It was a west wind so he had to sail way out and the mainsheet caught on a piling and the boat went over. It didn't completely sink. It didn't just wallow, either; it filled up with water to the cockpit. Peter was so proud of their accomplishment in winning this trophy that he just wasn't paying attention. In those days you had to pump the boats out with those old galvanized hand pumps. Even then the Mantoloking Yacht Club didn't have an electric pump.*

—Bob O'Brien

LOTUS OWNERS	
Bob Truitt	*1925–1930*
Fernand Schoettle	*1931–1946*
Ed Schoettle	*1947–1952*
Fred Winkelman	*1953–1958*
Russ Lord	*1959–1963*
Peter Kellogg/Dave McShane	*1964–1971*
Richard Macco	*1972–1973*
Brit Applegate	*1973–1974*
Nelson Hartranft	*1974–1976*
Toms River Seaport Society/Magierski	*1977–1982*
Steven Brick	*1983–2005*

Peter Kellogg

I first got involved with this thing when I was 18, when Dave McShane and I bought the *Lotus*. Usually, when you launch a boat, it floats. When they put *Lotus* in the water, it went directly toward the bottom and never stopped. This was a terrifying experience. And still we sailed the boat.

So we had that terrible first year of *Lotus*, it used to sink on us every time. I spent at least half the next summer underneath the boat—I'm sure I'm going to die early, having used a belt sander to get all that

Lotus *out of the water, showing the underwater profile of an A Cat. Notice how far the rudder extends.*

old copper off. Then we put caulk in the seams, that black stuff. We actually painted the bottom with this rubberized paint or something like that. I don't know what it was. But *Lotus* leaked a lot less, that did make a difference. And then we got to use battery-operated bilge pumps, which was a good innovation.

More bad luck for Lotus. *The young crew doesn't look at all fazed by the broken mast.*

Wasp | *Built in: 1980* | *Built for and currently owned by: Nelson Hartranft* | *Designer: Francis Sweisguth*
Builder: Beaton's Boatyard, West Mantoloking, New Jersey | *Sail number: 0 67*

WASP

Nelson Hartranft

How I got the *Wasp* is that a fellow by the name of Bob Scarborough had a big old schooner at the Cedar Point Yacht Club. It was tied up on the bulkhead there across from the yacht club building at the mouth of the entrance to the marina. I had a boat that I kept there. Bob brought that big old schooner in for the winter to be worked on. One of the guys who was working on the restoration happened to go into that antique shop that used to be on Route 9. The guy opened up a chest of drawers there and found the plans for an A Cat. Absolutely amazing.

So he took them to Fellows, Reed and Weber, the engineers. One of my buddies from Ocean Gate, a fellow by the name of Snapper Applegate, was working for them at the time, got ahold of a copy of the plans, and told me about them.

I had been talking to Lolly Beaton before that about the possibility of building an A Cat but he was sort of hesitant because he didn't have all the drawings that he needed. He was quite familiar with all the A Cats because he's the guy who had repaired everything for me.

When I told him we found that set of plans, that gave him the ability to go ahead. He really did it, he said, for the benefit of his son, Tom, who he wanted to have the experience of building a new one from scratch. So Tom and Paul at Beaton's, along with Lolly's supervision, built the *Wasp*.

The nicest thing about an A Cat is a sunset sail. It doesn't get any better than that. Especially if you get the opportunity to sit in the sail—the human boom vang—with a beer. You're heading toward Seaside, but the sun is setting behind you. —Gary Stewart

WASP TROPHIES

Bay Championship
1982, 1983, 1984, 1988

Middleton Cup
1982, 1983, 1984, 1988, 1999

Sewell Cup
1982, 1984, 1988, 1989, 1991, 1993

Morgan Cup
1982, 1985, 1986, 1987, 1988, 1992

Challenge Cup
1983, 1985, 1990, 1992

Tom Beaton, builder of Wasp

I think I talked my father into it. It didn't take much convincing. He has a love for this stuff but he doesn't always let on. He believes in history and tradition, so I think he did it for that reason.

They are a lot of work for a 28-foot boat. There's a lot of structure to support the mast that far forward. You could build a 35-foot boat and probably do about the same amount of work.

The problem with the boats from the 1920s was they all leaked under the mast. I think they

Thank goodness Nelson built a new A Cat. —Peter Kellogg

always had this problem. And the advantage we had when we made the *Wasp*, was we knew where the weaknesses were so we kind of engineered the mast step and other things to support that extra load. It needed extra strength there. And it worked pretty well.

When we built the *Wasp* we worried about it being so much faster than the other boats. We were afraid a new boat might ruin the whole class. We weren't that concerned about overall weight or about trying to make it faster. So we built it very traditionally

Twenty years down the line, we're doing a whole different thing. We are making boats lighter, the rudders are fairer, the centerboards are sharper, and the rigging is lighter. Weight is a big factor.

Wasp tunes up before a BBYRA race with full main. Mary Ann (right) has one reef. It is always a guessing game how much sail to carry.

Mitchell Shivers at the helm.

Tamwock | *Built in: 1990* | *Built for: Peter Kellogg* | *Named for: original* Tamwock | *Current owner: Austin and Gwen Fragomen*
Designer: Charles D. Mower | *Builder: John Brady, Philadelphia Maritime Museum* | *Sail numbers: BH T, MC T, T, TW*
Rebuilt in 2003 by Bill de Rouville

TAMWOCK

Austin Fragomen

I think what attracted me was the grace and beauty of the boats. That caught my attention. My wife and I decided that this looked like an interesting thing to do, sailing A Cats. They are a lot of fun and provide a lot of camaraderie.

I'd like to see the fleet grow. Frankly, I'm not sure it will. That is a tough question because A Cats are a fairly expensive commodity. There's a limited number of people who sail on the bay. One of the problems with A Cats is they only sail them on Barnegat Bay and ideally what we need to do is to widen the A Cat fleet beyond our particular Barnegat Bay Yacht Racing Association. Because of that connection, the destiny of A Cats will be determined by the destiny of the BBYRA overall.

Participation has been shrinking and basically the association is really trying very hard, through various clubs, to make sure that we hang on to the junior sailors. We have great junior sailors, but getting them to move up and sail as young adults and later on as people as old as me is not easily achieved. We take junior sailors out with us, in hopes of seriously interesting them. We do that regularly, not only in big point races, but for some of the local races run at Bay Head.

I own both *Witch* and *Tamwock*, and we're pretty competitive. Mike Frankovich and his team sail *Tamwock* and I sail on *Witch*. *Witch* is a little faster than *Tamwock*, so it is competitive, but *Witch* gets the better end of the parking most of the time.

Sailing A Cats takes a lot of forearm strength. That's the first thing. Great endurance. A strong back. I think that the biggest adaptation between these boats and sailing the J-boats, for instance, is that the A Cat boat is not going to turn on a dime. It doesn't handle like a dinghy. A J-24 essentially handles like dinghy. You can make the boat really do what you want. There has to be a lot more anticipation and a lot more foresight and planning with an A Cat. Can't wait until the last minute to maneuver.

The tiller on Fragomen's Tamwock.

part of that. I also got a hold of John Brady who was at the Maritime Museum. I'm not sure how I got connected with him. It may have been his idea to build an A Cat, actually, not mine.

Peter Kellogg

I think seeing *Wasp* in such terrific shape, looking so great, must have been what got me back, got me involved in the class again. And shortly after Hartranft did his renovation, the other boats started going through their rebuilding processes. So I think the excitement that Nelson put into it, showing what the possibilities were, all of that appealed to me.

Then when they took *Mary Ann* up to Maine, I helped fund

An A Cat doesn't look that big when you sail them, but when I saw the hull all opened up, and stood at either end and looked through it, all 28 feet right there before they put the deck on—I found that scary, overwhelming.

—Peter Kellogg

Russ Lucas

I was crewing on *Tamwock* for Jimmy Kellogg, sailing along. We always talk about one of the fun things in sailing is you always have to prep yourself for trouble, look out for trouble when things are going well. So we're sailing along toward Lavallette. We're about to run aground, so we're about to tack onto port and hit the layline.

Just before we tacked, I looked over and noticed that on our leeward upper, the shackle

One thing that just astounds me is how deeply people care about these boats. My dad's school buddy was Al Diss, who was the owner of Tamwock. *After* Tamwock *burned down, he named all his other sailboats* Tamwock. *I sailed on one of his* Tamwocks *for the Bermuda Race one time. I called him up and said by the way I was building a new A Cat and I wanted to name it* Tamwock, *but I wanted to make sure that was alright with him. He said he was delighted. The next week, a box showed up at the house and even though he had retired and moved to Florida, he'd saved all the BBYRA flags that* Tamwock *had won, including these night race flags. Night races were a big deal.*

—Peter Kellogg

had come undone and was just floating off in the breeze. It was just a freak of good luck that I noticed it.

But then, what do you do? You have all these people. You have an old wooden boat. How do you get out of this? We were able to quickly go anchor, drop the sail, and remain calm while we got another shackle going. We had a very good lead at that point, and we were able to fix it and still come in second, which was a lot of fun.

TAMWOCK OWNERS

Peter Kellogg	*1987–1997*
Mike Tufariello, Cory Wingerter,	
Peter Stagaard, Dave Alldian	*1998–1999*
Mitch Shivers/Austin Fragomen	*2000–2001*
Austin & Gwen Fragomen	*2000–2005*

Jimmy Kellogg, nephew of Peter Kellogg

I was first formally introduced to the A Cats through my uncle, Peter. He had owned and raced *Lotus* in the

I was working on my own boat during the winter of 1987, when John Brady had begun Tamwock. *I was smitten from the beginning. Every chance John gave me to work on her, I did, with joy. Peter Kellogg invited several of us for a sail, as a thank-you for everyone's efforts. I love boats, and I love sailing, but this A Cat stuff was entirely different. I couldn't get enough and basically wormed my way into a crew position for the next three racing seasons. They were wonderful, heady days, and I have never forgotten the thrill of a blustery downwind match with* Mary Ann, *booms outstretched, crews' nerves taught, John at the helm, calm as could be. It was so exhilarating! As a consequence of those precious days racing in the A Cat fleet, I have regained that childhood exuberance of sailing. I thank* Tamwock, *Peter, and John for that gift.*   —Suzanne Leahy, boat builder

'60s. Years later, he reentered the fleet with a tub of a boat, *Tamwock*, a reiteration of the original *Tamwock*. Tub or not, it was his pride and joy. And as such I took a shine to it, often borrowing it for pleasure sailing when he wasn't racing it. It turned out it was much more fun as a pleasure sailer then a racer.

I once borrowed *Tamwock* for a romantic weekend and took it on an overnight down bay. I had brought a little hibachi, upon which we cooked steaks off the back. I thought that was pretty cool, till the next morning. I realized that not only had I bubbled the varnish, I had also charred the wood black as coal, a good inch deep.

This did little to dampen my spirits, it being a beautiful morning. Pulling anchor and raising the massive sail, coasting out of Applegate Cove, this was truly a glorious time, when you had the whole bay to yourself, sun glinting off the water all around you—and a companion in a bikini.

But my uncle, with his usual early morning zeal,

using his signature sixth sense for checking up on errant nephews, soon appeared on the horizon in *Tradition*, come to check on his charge. You can be sure the cooler now covered the black spot of infamy! I had hoped (in vain) to repair the deck to its previous splendor unnoticed.

Pete Stagaard, *former owner of* Tamwock

My other partners on the boat and I are all Metedeconk River Yacht Club members, and one day we were talking and Dave Alldian brings up the subject of A Cats. Peter Kellogg had the *Tamwock*, and it was available for $45,000. It was a cheap way to get some experience in the fleet. Unfortunately, it was a brutal boat to sail and we never went anywhere. In that boat, you're always in the back third.

John Brady

We've built four A Cats, *Tamwock*, *Vapor*, *Spy II*, and *Torch*. And yes, we've learned from each one. That is reflected in their racing record. They are difficult to build—all the builders would agree on that. The boat doesn't make sense from an engineering standpoint. It is a really wide platform with a big stick. It just wants to twist itself apart. That's been the challenge, I think, since the first one was built.

Buzz Reynolds stands at the shrouds after Tamwock *capsizes on the starting line. Steve Tyler is still at the helm. Does this crew look like it is having a good time?*

John Brady, the builder, had conspired with my uncle to keep the old character of the A Cats intact: large wood blocks sparsely adorned the rig, with practically hemp rope for a halyard. Electric bailers had not yet been introduced, nor had the different tonnage of the various boats been taken into account. Tamwock *was clearly the heaviest.* —Jimmy Kellogg

Ghost | *Built in: 1994* | *Built for and currently owned by: Bill Fortenbaugh* | *Designer: Francis Sweisguth*
Builder: Beaton's Boatyard, West Mantoloking, New Jersey | *Sail number: BH G*

GHOST

Bill Fortenbaugh, *current owner of* Ghost

I capsized the first year. Beaton didn't have the boat ready and we wanted to sail the first Bay race. We were totally naïve. It is hard to imagine how ignorant we were. It was blowing and we went out there without seats in the boat and without foot braces on the floor. We were slipping all over the place. And on one occasion I slipped, and the boat heeled a bit too much, and down we went.

The second time, it was again blowing hard at Toms River and we did a jibe at I guess a reaching mark and we just rolled over. That was real beginner's stuff. But we saw *Bat* tip over the next year, doing exactly the same thing, so I felt better. I'm not the only one who has tipped one over by a long shot.

My biggest thrill in the A Cat actually happened after we were demoted to sort of the middle of the fleet in 2002. We went down to Little Egg, and we were just plain smarter than everybody. Both morning races we went south realizing the southerly was going to come in, and we won the regatta.

Dan Crabbe

Bill Fortenbaugh and I sort of co-skipper *Ghost*. He lets me sail probably a third to half the races. Up until about four years ago, for a period of seven or eight years after the *Ghost* was built, he won many many races, he dominated the Bay, winning five or six Bay Championships.

In recent years we've struggled, but we are coming back. *Ghost* was built, I guess, in the late '80s, and the new ones that were built later than that were much lighter. Both Philadelphia Seaport and Beaton's learned to make them lighter, so now we weigh them all and we make them all come up to a minimum weight by adding lead in specific places. That really has made them a lot more equal in speed. And it is noticeable. We'll go out there and race this summer with nine or ten races on the bay, and you'll have eight different winners.

And it gets close. This last time it came down right to the last race, the Seaside race, between the

I'll give you the honest answer. I tipped over one too many times in an E Scow and realized that I wasn't going to be a good E Scow sailor. So I looked around on Barnegat Bay and I saw the A Cats and they were so beautiful. That's the true answer. I looked at them as a retirement boat in which high tech did not exist.
—Bill Fortenbaugh

Witch and the *Spy*, for points. The boats that were third, fourth, and fifth weren't that far behind. That makes it nice when everybody shares in winning. It encourages them to come out and race.

The only comparison I know to E Scows is sailing downwind. Getting the boat balanced is extraordinarily important. In fact, the only place Ghost *is fast is downwind. It has never been fast upwind. The Mary Ann is the fastest boat upwind. It is the true Mower design, deeper than the rest. When the wind is up, I think it is unbeatable upwind. If it is well sailed I mean. But downwind* Ghost *has a very flat bottom and if we roll it ever so little to windward, get that mainsail up in the air, it goes very well downwind.*

—Bill Fortenbaugh

Bill Fortenbaugh concentrates intently at the helm of Ghost.

It's a very physically oriented boat and people don't always think of it that way when they build one. Bill Fortenbaugh is a great sailor and he came out of the E Scow fleet, and he thought the A Cat would be his retirement boat. I remember talking with him on the dock, I said, "Bill this boat will kill you." He now tells me I was right but he had a very successful run, he won the Bay Championship seven times in a row! But now he has realized it is much more fun to be a crewmember than it is to hold on to that tiller.

—Gary Stewart

Jimmy Kellogg at the helm. Note the bend of the boom. The crew looks to be flying over the water.

Vapor | *Built in: 1994* | *Built for and currently owned by: Peter Kellogg* | *Named for: first winner of the Challenge Cup*
Designer: Charles D. Mower | *Builder: John Brady, Philadelphia Ship Preservation Guild* | *Sail numbers: BH V, V*

VAPOR

***Jimmy Kellogg, skipper of* Vapor**

The anchor start race is a classic A Cat tradition, run out of Ocean Gate. We would sit up in their cramped bar for our skipper's meeting, and draw straws for the line up in front of the club. Many times an A Cat wound up beached on the shore if they weren't lucky enough to draw the best straw! All kind of tricks were employed, including shock cord on the anchor lines, extra long hawsers, and plain old trying to cheat the line.

One thing that makes the A Cats so special is that due to their beamy size, they are great for young kids. When not sailing in Bay races, the A Cats are loved by kids. To go sailing on the A Cats is a treat. They line up and down the boom, swing from the rigging in jury-rigged seats, or tow behind. And having two or more A Cats racing, each one swarming with kids, is a sight to behold! On a good day, it's possible to get 20 or more juniors on one A Cat.

Special events add to the magic of the A Cat fleet, like designing our yearly "Team Vapor" T-shirts, thinking about a bigger battle flag, or considering tie-dying the entire sail. In fact, Team Vapor took to meeting in a Mexican restaurant in Hoboken in the off-season to come up with some of our more outrageous ideas. During this time, Team Vapor decided that next year would be "The Year of the Yellow Submarine."

The race started with Peter Kellogg at the helm, executing a classic Peter Kellogg signature maneuver of splitting and threading the fleet while on port from behind the line.

—Stan Switlik

Jimmy Kellogg's children: Emily, Jimmy, and Grace.

We promptly painted the boat school-bus yellow, and had T-shirts made detailing the famous Beatles album cover.

Peter Kellogg

I think what our fleet needs to be doing is getting more juniors out on the boats. We do take the boats to the different clubs near the end of the season and try to get all their juniors out. We've had 40 kids or more out on these boats, sitting on the boom or whatever. Just to give them a sense of what it's like to actually be on one. I know when you are a kid growing up, A Cats are quite a sight.

Improvements have definitely been made, and these boats don't seem to come apart like they used to. It is no longer a bailing job. You used to spend your time sailing around, bailing. I'll never forget when I went out on the *Bat* for the first time, I hadn't been on an A Cat for years. I didn't know quite what to do. I do know as soon as we went around the weather mark, I ran down below to start pumping, and there was no water in the bilge. I was just astounded. That is a big difference in the boats. It makes it so much more fun.

John Brady

We did *Vapor* over one winter with five people. *Vapor* was fun to build because it was very focused. Building fast really obliges you to stick to the plan.

<table>
<tr><td colspan="2" align="center">VAPOR TROPHIES</td></tr>
<tr><td align="center">*Middleton Cup* 1996</td></tr>
<tr><td align="center">*Sewell Cup* 1995, 2003</td></tr>
<tr><td align="center">*Challenge Cup* 1998, 1999</td></tr>
</table>

Jenny Buck (right) assists on main trimming. Garet Veerland trims the main and Jimmy Kellogg is at the helm.

Vapor's *crew, including Sherri de Rouville in the blue shirt, hikes hard after rounding the leeward mark.*

We've obviously had some of those hot shot E Scow sailors come sail with us. It is a tough transition for them. —Peter Kellogg

Raven | *Built in: 2001* | *Built for and currently owned by: Mike Turfariello, Cory Wingerter, Peter Stagaard, Dave Alldian*
Designer: Francis Sweisguth | *Builder: Beaton's Boatyard, West Mantoloking, New Jersey* | *Sail number: MC R*

RAVEN

Peter Stagaard, owner of **Raven**

When you are trying to go downwind, there is enough sail on that boat so that it can push the bow right down, almost submarine the boat. You really have to move people back in the boat, get them off the cabin top. Keep the back end of the boat down because there is so much sail on it. Just overpowered. That's the scariest. The idea of that big boom coming uncontrolled through the cockpit with all those people. I mean that would just be a killer.

If it is out of control, you're kind of holding the mast up with the running backstay. If the boom comes across and slams right on it, it is going to break it. People tend to try to lock the backstay on when there is a lot of pressure. You've got to put a lot of muscle into it to relieve that backstay.

Mike Tufariello, owner of **Raven**

What is nice about the class now is they've gotten a lot more organized. They are really trying to make it fair, make it more toward one-design sailing. Then it shows you a few more things about the people on the boat, the character of the individuals, when everything else is about the same level.

With a J-24 you have a lot more things going on, more you can tweak and a lot more sails you can use. But it is still the prowess of the tactician . . . still your basics. So when it gets down to it, it is how long the crew has been together and how well they work together. Mechanically, the boats are different but other than that, to make them win it is the same formula.

Is Raven *clear of barrel F? The crew wisely doesn't look.*

Jim Gelenitis, Raven *sailor*

Hopes were high for the owners and crew of Metedeconk's black boat when the 2004 sailing season began. Although light and fast, *Raven* had proven to be inconsistent, particularly in heavy air.

To address this problem, a new mast was ordered and a newer sail rigged. But even with the upgrades the boat could not break into the top three over the first weeks of the BBYRA series.

Frustrated, the crew played with the rig, tightening, loosening, and tightening again. Sails were changed, photographed, and analyzed. Measurements were taken and compared to other boats. Nothing seemed to work or shed light on the problem.

The fifth race of the BBYRA series—the Challenge Cup—sailed out of Toms River Yacht Club. Nothing out of the ordinary was done to prepare the boat. Immediately after the start the

We were trying to come up with a name, also trying to come up with a color for the hull. The fleet itself has all these simple names, one syllable, the Bat, *the* Ghost, *the* Spy, *and we wanted to keep ours simple. We decided on the black hull and then we toyed with other names like the* Witch *and things of the occult, and then the idea of the* Raven *came along. Somebody threw it out and we all liked it.*

—Pete Stagaard

pre-race favorites *Spy* and *Witch* jumped to an early lead. The rest of the fleet trailed with *Raven* firmly ensconced in mid-fleet, a spectator again to race events. As the fleet sailed north on the last run to barrel F at the foot of the Mathis Bridge, the wind eased noticeably and the fleet, once spread over the leg, began to bunch. At the same time, the two lead boats engaged in a series of luffing matches that permitted the fleet to close in even further.

As *Spy* and *Witch* approached barrel F the two leaders became entangled and sailed past the mark, permitting the next two boats, *Torch* and *Ghost*, to squeeze inside and into the lead. *Raven* somehow also managed to slip by the one-time leaders as

The boats ahead always look a long way off . . .

they untangled, and slid into third place with two legs to go.

In all the excitement *Raven* was about to follow the leaders when a voice on the boat piped in: "Are you sure they're sailing to the right mark?" After a second of stunned silence there was a mad dash for the course sheet—sure enough, there was an obscure provision in the racing instructions that the A Cat fleet disregard the last mark on a barrel course and instead round a fluorescent green inflatable mark nicknamed the "schmoo" by the race committee. *Raven* rounded first followed closely by *Torch* and *Spy*. The last leg was a water-borne game of ping-pong as the *Raven* was forced to cover both trailing boats, which split to different sides of the course. *Raven* finally crossed the line no more than one boat length ahead of *Torch*, unexpectedly winning the Challenge Cup.

The funny thing about this story is what happened afterward. No one fiddled with the rig tension. The same sail was used. No new go-fasts were added and the grumbling stopped. Over the course of the summer, the boat went on to win the Newman Trophy, the Middleton Cup, and the Sewell Cup.

As it turned out, it was never the boat that was the problem.

You do feel as if the boat belongs on the bay. When you look at other A Cats, and you realize what type of boat you're on, well, it gives you a good feeling about sailing, about the area, and about how you are enjoying your free time.
—Mike Turfariello

Cory Wingerter

When I was 10 years old I was asked to sail on *Mary Ann*, which had a whole bunch of holes in it. All I remember was being down below, pumping.

There was no A Cat representation from Metedeconk so a bunch of us guys got together

With the crew sitting in and the boat upright, the crew of Raven *is thinking of unreefing the sail.*

and bought *Tamwock*. We weren't happy with the performance so we pooled our resources and had Beaton build us *Raven*.

Peter Kellogg is really the guy behind all of this. He built *Tamwock* in Philadelphia and we just loved the boat. We liked the atmosphere. We also try to have kids and women on the boat, which we think is a good thing.

In my opinion, we have gotten a little more serious and that is why we've done better. People have to know their jobs on the boat. We have four owners and last year we decided to have one helmsman. That was a big help instead of having the owners change off. I don't need to steer. I just enjoy going out there. Peter has been our helmsman and it has worked out very well.

David Alldian, owner of Raven

After doing a lot of regattas elsewhere and then having a family, I liked the idea that I was going to be able to take my kids on these boats because they were so close. It is a day trip, not a three- or four-day event. And I was really interested in the history of this fleet.

I think the one thing that is pretty amazing is that in today's fleet we have 10, 11, or 12 boats showing up every Saturday. You actually have a hundred people out there every weekend sailing these things. And then there is the support crew that goes along with the chase boats and everything.

After each Saturday race they have trophies and there's an award ceremony and there is all the camaraderie that goes along with that.

Spy II | *Built in: 2001* | *Built for and currently owned by: Jane Wilkins, Roy Wilkins, Maggie Groff, Gary Stewart, Richard Yetman,*
Gale Yetman | *Designer: Francis Sweisguth* | *Builder: John Brady, Independence Seaport Museum, Philadelphia, Pennsylvania*
Sail number: IH SPY

SPY II

Gary Stewart

A Cats exist simply because there is a group of people that have a love of the tradition on Barnegat Bay. It absolutely makes you feel connected to the area.

It takes teamwork more than anything else. If you don't have a tremendous afterguard, a mainsheet man, and also a captain of the boat who organizes everything, well, you can't steer one of these things and race it well. I always suggest to people that it's the only boat I've ever sailed that will sail itself and take control of you. A lot of times you can't look around because the boat is a monster to sail if it gets to be any kind of wind. So if your team doesn't really know what they are doing, all of them, then you are just going to be in trouble.

Initially, I was the tactician for a long time and Roy drove. Back then, I thought we were very, very dangerous around the racecourse in that way because it allowed me to look around. Roy is a tremendous helmsman. And even now I drive upwind and he drives downwind because I'm just not physically strong enough sometimes to control that thing. You do get exhausted. A Cats go over these 10-mile courses and so Roy basically takes the tiller at the windward mark and he's great downwind. Then I'm completely fresh at the leeward mark again and then we can really rock and roll. I think a lot more of the boats are tending to do that. But you also have to have two helmsmen that are just really good. We have three, with Richard Yetman as our mainsheet main.

The *Spy* team is very family-oriented. Some of our competitors look like a professional football team when they come down on the dock. We have a bunch of kids and if you're family, you sail with us. We don't bring linebackers on board and we still do very well.

The annual Wilkins Thanksgiving Day sail.

My most horrifying moment might have been last season. We were tied for the lead in the Challenge Cup with Russell Lucas, neck and neck coming into the second-to-last mark, and there was an issue with an overlap and he had to go behind us and he clipped our stern. It spun us out, and it spun him out, and I just really thought that very easily could have been the end, with all the booms flying around and everything else. Luckily it wasn't.

Roy Wilkins

I guess I became an organizer because I have coached all my life. I just sort of take charge of things. The class was in disarray and, being a coach, I'm very adamant about fair play. I saw the direction the A Cats were going, the class was becoming very unequal. All I wanted when I was a soccer coach was a level playing field. I just tried to do the same thing

Richard Yetman, Gary Stewart, Roy Wilkins, Maggie Groff, and Andrew Groff.

The trailing boats block the wind of the leaders, tightening up the race.

in sailing. It's been extremely difficult, but I think I've finally achieved my ultimate goal. All the boats are even, and the racing is very exciting right now. In 2003, seven different boats won individual races. In 2004, six boats finished first in separate races. There is no other class on the bay that can say that.

Jane Wilkins, owner of Spy

It all started for the Wilkins family in 1978 when we purchased *Spy* with our dear friends Charlie and Donna Cox. We wanted a boat that would best fit our family and an A Cat came to mind. We spent many a family evening sailing on the river, enjoying

SPY TROPHIES

Bay Championship 2001, 2004

Sewell Cup 2001

Morgan Cup 2001

Challenge Cup 2001, 2002, 2003

I have taken a significant number of friends sailing on our boat. And they are just amazed at the workmanship, the size of the sail, the detail in the woodwork, how fast it can go. You don't think this big, heavy, fat boat is going to go very fast. They are just shocked when it does, and are always in awe of the beauty of the craftsmanship of those boats. —Maggie Groff

the sunsets with the kids. We raced for the next two years until *Spy* literally fell apart. Beaton's allowed Roy to work on the boat in their yard in order to keep the cost of fixing her down, but the Cox's were moving and we needed new partners. J.T. Reynolds and Maggie Groff joined our cause. Roy spent weekends for two years in Beaton's working on *Spy*.

Once the rebuild was complete we had a new family to enjoy *Spy*, including the Reynolds and Groff families. We had many different crews through the years. Chris Chadwick was a "young stud" who we invited

River Dixon and the Challenge Cup.

to be our mainsheet man. He was only 16 when he began his career on cats. He is now the father of three daughters and is still racing. A young, long-haired law student named Gary Stewart joined our team in 1990. He is now like a brother to us, married to Christel with a daughter. We spend many a summer evening with them and Maggie and her husband, Richard. Cats just seem to bring people together. Fran Brady, our mainsheet man for a time, is also a partner.

The building of *Spy ll* in 2000 brought the Yetman family to the team, our dearest friends for over 25

Of course our first Bay Championship was exhilarating. Every Bay Championship is, but I have to say, you know how important the Challenge Cup is to Gary Stewart. He has a magnificent way of getting us all as excited about the Challenge Cup as he is. Not this past summer, but the summer before when we won the Challenge Cup, the weather was just unbelievable. They cut the race short because the weather was so severe. Things like that, moments like that are the ones that you really remember.   —Maggie Groff

years. We have had so many special moments on *Spy*, like our daughter's wedding and racing for the Bay Championship in 2004 when it came to the last race. Roy and Gary decided that we would carry the same amount of crew as the *Witch* (that we were tied with for the championship). As *Witch* took crew off the boat we had to decide which crew member would go. Immediately Tyler Yetman, the youngest, said it would not be him and the fighting among the younger set began until Roy said that since we all got us there no one was leaving. We won, but it was when many said it was so nice to see a "family boat" win the Bay that the real victory hit me.

Now we have *Spy* grandchildren. They are yet too young to race, but if anyone mentions an outing on *Spy* it is an immediate, "me too!" They walk the

Spy *team displays the Bay Championship flag at the awards ceremony, Seaside Park Yacht Club, 2004.*

decks as if they own the bay. Roy and I are fortunate enough to know that in time of need, any A Cat sailor would be their for us, and that we would be there for them.

From left: Jake Schmierer, Doug D'Alessandro, Jim Urner, Peter Chance, Willy de Camp, Peter Kellogg at helm, Timo White.

Torch | *Year Built: 2002* | *Built for and currretly owned by: Peter Kellogg* | *Designer: Francis Sweisguth*
Builder: John Brady, Independence Seaport Museum, Philadelphia, Pennsylvania | *Sail numbers: T, Torch*

TORCH

Peter Kellogg

When you think about competitiveness, you have to go back to when I was 18 and the fleet would finish a barrel length apart. The only boat that was "competitive" was the last boat to have gotten fixed up. With manila lines, cotton sails, and galvanized pumps, this wasn't racing, it was survival, a drowning match trying to keep the water out.

When I first bought *Lotus*, the committee would ask us, the day after a race, whether we had finished, because they would have abandoned it—we'd be four barrel lengths behind and they had wanted to go home. Which they did. We used to finish with the water in the bilge over our knees. It was madness.

But I think with all the boats being new, now we all finish within a short time period, which to me is a big deal. Sometimes it ends up that there is a fleet up in the front and a fleet in the back. But I think each boat in the fleet is capable of winning today. Two years ago, I think we had seven different boats, out of a possible ten, come in first. What else can you ask for? I think that is unbelievable.

Glen Dickson, Barnegat Bay sailor

On my first sail aboard *Torch*, I got the chance to drive the boat out from its mooring at Island Heights Yacht Club. Peter Chance and foredeck man Stan Switlik tuned the rig, tightening the lowers to make sure the mast was straight. I had never steered an A Cat before, and my first impression was that it was like driving a big, powerful bus; I had to brace my foot against the centerboard trunk to get enough leverage to fight the weather helm. It was only blowing about 12 knots from the east and we had seven people aboard, but the boat felt overpowered. We had just tacked onto starboard,

Joe Mignon (left), Peter Chance (blue shirt), and Stan Switlik (far right).

Peter Kellogg celebrates winning the Bay Championship with Gary Stewart (middle) and Richard Yetman (r).

right in the middle of the Wanamaker course, when trimmer Sam Earle brought the mainsail in a bit more, which further loaded up the helm.

Peter took over the tiller to check the boat's feel and sailed about five boatlengths before I heard the loudest bang I've ever heard on a boat. I looked up to see the mast collapsing to leeward—it had broken about two feet above the deck.

The boat came upright pretty rapidly, and I heard shouts of "man overboard!" and looked down to see Stan blowing by at about four knots. I reached down and grabbed him, and someone else helped me pull him out of the water. Sam was also in the water. He had seen the mast bow to leeward in a big "C" shape before it broke. We spent the next half hour pulling in the massive sail and getting the big Sitka spruce mast back aboard,

Peter Wright (with green hat and white shirt) tends mainsheet.

The boats have been going through a real growth spurt in terms of rules, figuring out how to keep any changes within bounds. I think if you look at all the different boats, you will find different approaches on how to overcome the physical problems. We did the rig exactly as it was drawn by Mower. The neat thing about that was we found out why every change was made. It was things like the jumper strut was much longer in the original plan but it turned out that if you built it that way, it tended to create an "s." There was too much compression on the mast, and it actually pushed the mast aft at the spreader. My latest approach on the hulls has been to use laminated web frames on either side to stiffen them, combined with bond strapping, both of which are pretty old concepts. I guess if I had another one to do I might refine that a little more. I think I have the basic idea down. But another builder might do a boat that changes my thinking about it completely.

—John Brady

lashed to the boom. Soon we were picked up by Peter Kellogg's 35-foot RIB, "White Whale," and recounting stories of the break.

The root of the failure: a titanium shackle that connected the starboard lower to the spreader had broken, leaving the mast unsupported. The mast quickly bent and then snapped right at the top of the solid mast plug. Fortunately, no one was hurt. Despite the setback, *Torch* was back racing the next Saturday with its spare mast.

Torch being towed back in after breaking its mast.

Austin Fragomen and Russell Lucas share the helm of Witch. *Brent Wagner, trimming the mainsail, helped build the boat at the de Rouville yard.*

Witch | *Year Built: 2002* | *Built for and currently owned by: Austin and Gwen Fragomen* | *Designer: Francis Sweisguth*
Builder: de Rouville Boat Shop, Cedar Creek, New Jersey | *Sail number: W*

WITCH

Austin Fragomen, owner of Witch

Our biggest competition has been *Spy*. For the last three years the Bay Championship was decided in the last race in terms of where we finish and where *Spy* would finish.

The strategy must be to know where you are in the fleet, and not get yourself into situations in close quarters. These boats cannot be sailed, or should not be sailed, overly aggressively, because of their weight and size of their boom. You could argue that the racing is maybe a little more aggressive than it should be, considering the nature of the boat.

Bill de Rouville, builder of Witch

The special challenge for us was that we had never done it before. We had done some repair and service work on a number of A Cats, but we hadn't built one in our shop. It was a challenge to build a boat that would be aesthetically pleasing and competitive. And competitive is important, in that fleet.

Racing the boats makes me constantly aware of the different stresses that get placed on things. Sometimes it is through failure. We'll have a fitting fail or have an item fail, then we realize it needs to be either a little beefier or engineered a little differently. There is always a learning process going on.

With the A Cat you can have different generations aboard. Doug Love, who has sailed on the bay forever, is a very important tactician. He is great as the afterguard, being able to say, "You are as far right as you are ever having to go. In my 40 years of racing, the breeze has never gone farther right on a day like this."
—Russ Lucas

WITCH TROPHIES

Bay Championship 2002

Sewell Cup 2005

Morgan Cup 2002, 2003, 2004, 2005

Challenge Cup 2005

Russ Lucas, helmsman on Witch

Part of the fun of sailing on Barnegat Bay is knowing where you are going to run aground. There are a lot of obstacles. Do you know how far west you should go before everybody starts running aground? It is like performing a lot of chess moves—where you try to force your better competition into these geographically bad places, and then catch the highest part of the lane that would keep you going to the west where you know the sea breeze is going to cycle over to the right as the day goes on.

A Cats are like big boats, where the guys behind get to strategically control the boats in front by trying to herd them together. There is a lot more match racing going on during the year in terms of boat-on-boat competition.

And it is always fun where the boats are the personalities not the skippers. There's *Bat*, here comes *Ghost*. It's not like here's Kellogg and here's Fortenbaugh. It truly is the boat. You are only talking about the boat.

Every club on Barnegat Bay is trying to find a way to get their juniors to transition to be on the bay for life. Toward that end, we continue to hope someday to have one A Cat per club as a minimum. It is crucial to the bay that A Cats really continue to thrive. They are almost a two- or three-season boat as they are very dry and you can sail them in the spring and fall. With one reef, you can sail them in any breeze, so they really are fun. And fun at cocktail hour as well.

It just goes to the point that we are so lucky to be on Barnegat Bay. Safe water. We don't have to do overnights. We don't have to buy keelboats. The owner gets to skipper.

A Cats, like every boat, sail better when you find the right blend of pressure and helm. We have found two main areas that make a substantial improvement in the helm and subsequent speed of *Witch*.

Upwind, as the wind increases above 15–18, we begin to heel too much. We always have a fair

number of women, thus a lighter-than-normal crew. As we become overpowered, we find that by "playing" the board we can find a sweet spot in the helm that is very fast. In high winds, this is very fast. Rather than rocking up and down in wind and waves, a little less board allows me to lock the boat

Austin and Gwen Fragomen (wearing white hats) on Witch. *There is never a bad day on an A Cat.*

Gwen Fragomen (white cap and white shirt left of center) and her team racing the Women's Worlds.

Witch almost comes to a stop in the chop.

Witch's cockpit.

into a groove, foot toward our favored side of the course and go faster through the water without sliding as much to leeward.

Downwind, our generation of A Cat sailors has been raised seeing the glorious pictures of crewmembers lounging on the boom, acting as a human vang. We feel like we made a major breakthrough by moving past this tradition, focusing all of our crew weight on the widest part of the beam, typically standing up to crowd the weight together. I move this "mass" forward and aft to balance the helm and bow wave. Having a crewmember on the boom never really kept the boom any flatter, like a good vang should. What it really did was put extra pressure on the leeward side of the boat to create more helm. In all but the biggest winds, we can sail lower and faster than other boats. In the big winds, we do put someone on the boom. That at least helps control the boom in big puffs and the helm is less of an issue.

Compare the pre-race scene aboard Witch *to the picture on page nine. Have things really changed over the years?*

George Schuld, boat builder

Brent and I arrive together at the Mantoloking Yacht Club. It is a beautiful Sunday morning. The club is silent and empty. In fact, not a single person is to be seen. Not a surprise, really, since it is early in the spring and there are no races today. Soon Bill de Rouville and his wife Sheryl arrive. After a few brief words, we untie the boat, pull her out of the slip by hand, and carefully work our way around the dock to the south side and tie off the bow, letting the soft northeast breeze keep her into the wind and comfortably off the dock.

We work together putting on the sail as we have done many times before with these boats. But this time was different. We all knew it was different. A sail was going on this boat for the very first time. The three of us gave the boat a thorough looking over to see if we had overlooked anything and checked out the rig once more, probably more out of habit than

Torch, Witch, *and* Vapor *sailing off Little Egg Harbor.*

anything. About that time, Henry Colie arrived and completed our shorthanded shakedown crew roster. Once he was on board, we manned our stations and raised sail. Henry untied us from the dock and with a slight pushing of the bow to the west we were off.

The first sail of the *Witch* was the most pride-filled and satisfying sail of my life to date. And I'll wager it was for Bill and Brent as well. To the Fragomens—thank you . . . and go fast!

Lightning | *Year Built: 2003* | *Built for and currently owned by: Steven Brick* | *Designer: Francis Sweisguth*
Builder: Beaton's Boatyard, West Mantoloking, New Jersey | *Sail number: lightning bolt*

LIGHTNING

Steve Brick, owner of Lightning

Like any boat, winning takes a lot of practice and good communication between the mainsheet man and the person on the tiller, along with the rest of the crew. I should add the tactician in the mix: communication between the guy on the sheet and the tiller and the tactician. They have to be in sync.

I would say breaking a mast is the most horrifying. We've broken the mast twice. Although it comes down slowly, more slowly than you would think, it's a horrifying moment. It makes a very loud noise and, depending on the direction in which it falls, it's a harrowing situation. The most exhilarating moment would be the leeward mark rounding after a short downwind leg, after a short upwind leg and then a short downwind leg. The racing gets close

If the fleet has a challenge, it is that we have a lot of races. And everybody, or a great many of the yacht clubs, want to have a special race at their club, and people are attempting to stretch the season both in the spring and the fall. So it gets to be a lot.

The calendar is full and when you are coordinating eight people, it's busy. We have some fleet members who resolved not to sail on Sundays at all. I think the fleet needs to wrestle with this issue—we do have families who think we should be doing something other than sailing A Cats on occasion.

It is always a sense of accomplishment to round the windward mark. Lightning *takes the lead.*

Tom Beaton

The last few years, we've been doing more work on the rigs and trying to get the weight out of the end a little bit. Henry Colie is a big innovator of A Cat stuff, but I think we are getting close to where things are going to start breaking if they get much lighter.

Drew Seibert, Chairman, Ocean County College Sailing Advisory Board

A Cats are probably the most followed of all the BBYRA races. You're supposed to be assigned to a class when you are out doing the patrol. People put in their option in hopes of getting the A Cats so they can go out there and follow them around. Huge contingent. It is a good spectator fleet and quite a show sometimes. What with the screaming and the yelling.

Lightning bolt carved into cockpit.

THE YACHT CLUBS AND REGATTAS

Painting by Virginia Perle.

Barnegat Bay Yacht Racing Association

Bay Head Yacht Club | *Beachwood Yacht Club* | *Island Heights Yacht Club*

Lavallette Yacht Club | *Manasquan River Yacht Club*

Mantoloking Yacht Club | *Metedeconk River Yacht Club*

Normandy Beach Yacht Club | *Ocean Gate Yacht Club*

Pine Beach Yacht Club | *Seaside Park Yacht Club*

Shore Acres Yacht Club | *Toms River Yacht Club*

A whimsical illustration of Barnegat Bay, published by Henry H. Horrocks in 1932.

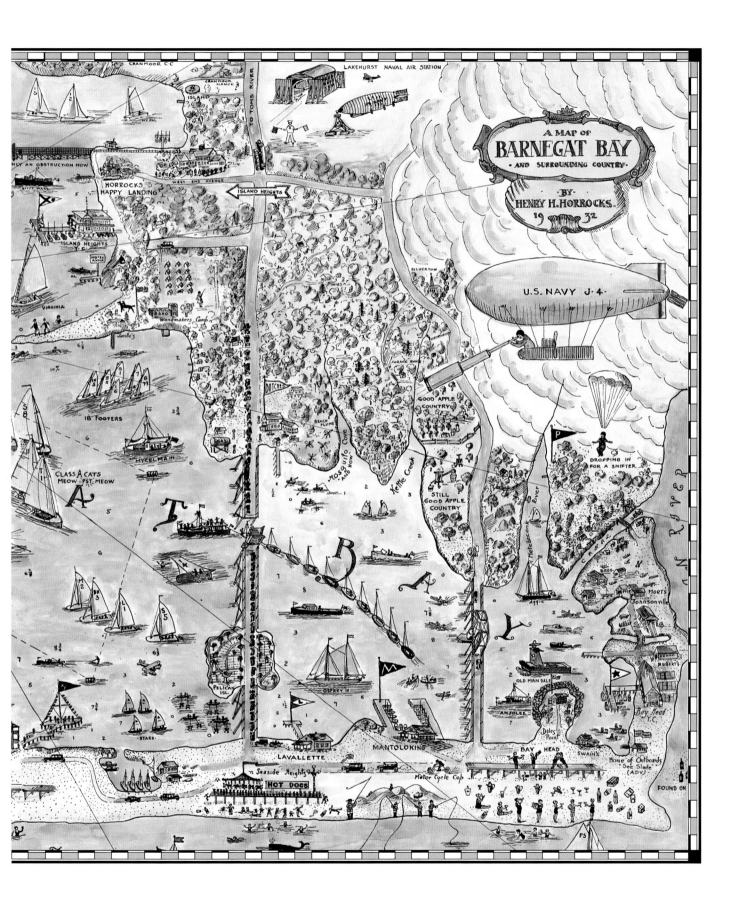

Even at rest, A Cats have a businesslike appearance. You can just sense the battle is yet to take place.

BARNEGAT BAY
Yacht Racing Association

It's extraordinary that so many yacht clubs occupy the precious waterfront property of Barnegat Bay. It would be virtually impossible to start one from scratch in today's regulatory, high-cost world. But happily, for thousands of members, 13 very unique clubs grace the shores of this 40-mile-long stretch of water.

By nature yacht clubs are tribal. I was intrigued to see Virginia Perle's fabulous watercolor paintings depicting the yacht clubs of Barnegat Bay. What an eclectic collection of architectural gems. Every club has its own personality. Members feel comfortable at their own clubs and, not surprisingly, rivalries develop on the racecourse, between junior programs, and at social gatherings. Of course, everyone believes their home club is the best. When someone is asked what club they belong to, watch how the answer arrives with pride.

Everyone knows that friendly rivalries are healthy, competition promotes excellence, and clubs learn from each other. This is what makes these yacht clubs great.

A Cats start off Island Heights Yacht Club racing for the Wanamaker Cup. All boats have one reef in this westerly breeze.

Since its development as a thriving summer resort area, and even before, sailing on Barnegat Bay has been a very popular sport. Racing sailboats from several yacht clubs had been competing with each other—and against workboats as well—many decades before 1914. But in 1914, Seaside Park Yacht Club's commodore, Herman Muller, called a meeting with members of three other yacht clubs (Bay Head, Island Heights, and Ocean Gate) to investigate organizing an association to both foster and unify yacht racing on Barnegat Bay.

The Barnegat Bay Yacht Racing Association (BBYRA) was founded at a time when large catboats

were the premiere class on the bay. The BBYRA organized a weekly racing circuit that survives to this day. These regattas are important because they bring sailors together to enjoy their cherished passion. And the bay should take a lot of pride in the outstanding junior talent developed at the BBYRA member clubs.

The first BBYRA race was held at Seaside Park Yacht Club on July 4, 1914. By the end of the first year, Mantoloking Yacht Club and Lavallette Yacht Club had also been added to the roster, and a "Racing Commission" was established to run regattas. In the following decades BBYRA expanded

its membership to include Toms River Yacht Club (1922), Shore Acres Yacht Club (1941), Beachwood Yacht Club (1946), Metedeconk River Yacht Club (1946), Normandy Beach Yacht Club (1947), Manasquan River Yacht Club (1962), and Pine Beach Yacht Club (1970).

After nearly a century of overseeing the many, many races on Barnegat Bay throughout the summer and on into frostbite season, the mission of the BBYRA has not changed. Fostering the sport on the bay and helping to organize the best races for the most boats is still the BBYRA's primary goal. The trophies they present are much sought after.

It makes me wonder if every club should one day have their own A Cat to send out into battle. This would certainly give every sailor a reason to cheer for their own team.

Barnegat Bay Championship

2005	*Raven*	1982–1984	*Wasp*	1969	*Lotus*	1937–1941	*Bat*
2004	*Spy II*	1981	*Mary Ann*	1968	*Mary Ann*	1936	*Tamwock*
2003	*Torch*	1980	*Bat*	1965–1967	*Spy*	1935	*Mary Ann*
2002	*Witch*	1979	*Mary Ann*	1964	*Mary Ann*	1934	*Bat*
2001	*Spy II*	1978	*Bat*	1962–1963	*Spy*	1933	*Mary Ann*
1994–2000	*Ghost*	1977	*Lotus*	1961	*Mary Ann*	1931–1932	*Bat*
1992–1993	*Mary Ann*	1976	*Spy*	1959–1960	*Spy*	1928–1930	*Tamwock*
1991	*Bat*	1975	*Bat*	1953–1958	*Lotus*	1927	*Spy*
1989–1990	*Spy*	1974	*Spy*	1952	*Spy*	1926	*Tamwock*
1988	*Wasp*	1972–1973	*Bat*	1951	*Bat*	1925	*Spy*
1986–1987	*Bat*	1971	*Lotus*	1950	*Spy*	1922–1924	*Mary Ann*
1985	*Spy*	1970	*Mary Ann*	1946–1949	*Bat*	1942–1945:	*no racing*

The Nelson R. Hartranft Trophy, donated to the Bay Head Yacht Club by Peter R. Kellogg in 1990, is in honor of Nelson Hartranft's many years of dedication to the A Cat class on Barnegat Bay. At one time, Nelson owned the Bat, *the* Spy, *the* Mary Ann *and the* Lotus. *He also had David Beaton & Sons build the* Wasp *to the plans and specifications of one of the original A Cats. The Nelson R. Hartranft Trophy is to be awarded each year at the Bay Head Yacht Club's Barnegat Bay Yacht Racing Association race day, to the winner of the A Cat class.*

The BBYRA kicks off the summer season at the Bay Head Yacht Club.

Nelson R. Hartranft Trophy

Year	Boat	Year	Boat	Year	Boat	Year	Boat	Year	Boat
2005	No Race	2002	*Witch*	1996	*Ghost*	1993	*Mary Ann*	1991	*Bat*
2004	*Witch*	2000	*Vapor*	1995	*Ghost*	1992	*Mary Ann*	1990	*Wasp*
2003	*Torch*	1999	*Wasp*	1994	*Vapor*	1997, 1998, 2001, 2005: *no racing*			

BAY HEAD
Yacht Club

Before 1870, few signs of human habitation were visible from a boat on the northern part of Barnegat Bay. But the lure of the ocean was irresistible, and soon entrepreneurial businesses, involving people mostly from the Princeton area, decided to create summer resorts in Bay Head and Mantoloking. These resorts flourished when the railroad provided access to the shore from both Philadelphia and New York. In the fall of 1888, a handful of residents of Bay Head got together with a purpose: to start a sailing club.

As one of the oldest yacht clubs in America, the Bay Head Yacht Club has flourished since its inception. The club has grown through four clubhouses; tennis was added in the early years, and after World War II, snack bar and restaurant facilities were added. The trophies that adorn the various display cases in the clubhouse and the flags hanging in the ballroom all attest to the prowess of Bay Head Yacht Club's sailors and tennis players.

Today, sailing, tennis, platform tennis, bridge, and other activities are enjoyed to the fullest by the active membership of approximately 875 families. The club has grown from a two-month-a-year, summer retreat to an almost year-round, full-service institution designed and managed to enhance the enjoyment of all members in the Bay Head/Mantoloking area. The Nelson R. Hartranft Trophy is awarded to the winning A Cat at Bayhead's BBYRA race each year.

Ed Vienckowski, A Cat sailor

I was privileged to be asked by Bill Fortenbaugh to be part of his team aboard *Ghost* when she was launched in 1994. On the morning of that first race, Tom Beaton and his team of skilled craftsmen scrambled to finish up as many last-minute details as they could. Seeing all that remained to make ready, I wondered at the prospect of our inaugural sail being our very first race for the season championship.

But Bill Fortenbaugh was determined to race that day on behalf of host Bay Head Yacht Club.

Certain concessions had to be made in order to sail that first race. Leaving the dock, we did not fully appreciate how much the absence of a detail like toerails in the cockpit might play into the day's events. But there was simply no time for their installation.

A classic Barnegat Bay sea breeze kicked in, and as the race wore on, the wind continued to build to upwards of 20 knots.

Bay Head Yacht Club.

Vapor in a big blow. Peter Kellogg, at the helm, is working hard to get the boat to bear off. The crewmember sitting in the cockpit looks lonely.

All A Cats are reefed on the starting line of the 2004 Worlds.

Without those toerails to bear against, handling the helm was a losing battle.

And then the ultimate humiliation occurred. Helping each other on the tiller through a brutal upwind leg, and already well behind the leaders, we capsized coming out of a tack. As far as I knew, this was the first time in decades that an A Cat had capsized during a race. I listened to Bill express his absolute sense of embarrassment, but at the same time saw a steely determination in his eyes. Based on the reaction from others to that first day's performance, it became apparent that *Ghost* was not being considered all that serious a contender.

Any such thinking was clearly misguided.

During the next week, all the unfinished details were completed, and we got an early start for the second race at Island Heights. That day, and for the rest of the year, Bill Fortenbaugh showed a competitive fire that I had never fully appreciated in my many years sailing against him in scows. *Ghost* went on to win every race in 1994, starting an incredible string of seven consecutive BBYRA championships.

Bill surely raised my game during my tenure in his afterguard, but perhaps more importantly, he forced others in the fleet to raise their game as well. As a result, the entire A Cat fleet is more competitive today than it has ever been. Bill Fortenbaugh clearly deserves much of the credit for that.

A Cat sailors compete for the Skip Moorhouse Trophy at Beachwood Yacht Club each year. The junior sailing program remains enthusiastic, and BYC has produced nationally and internationally known sailors, both men and women. Beachwood Yacht Club is the proud owner of "Woody," a restored duckboat donated by Peter Kellogg's generous restoration project.

The old Beachwood Yacht Club as it stood on the shores of the Toms River until 1981.

Skip Moorhouse Trophy

Year	Boat	Year	Boat	Year	Boat
2005	*Ghost*	1999	*Ghost*	1995	*Spy*
2004	*Spy II*	1998	*Ghost*	1994	*Ghost*
2001	*Spy II*	1997	*Ghost*	1991	*Spy*
2000	*Lotus*	1996	*Ghost*		

1992, 1993, 2002, 2003: no racing

BEACHWOOD
Yacht Club

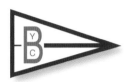

The Beachwood Yacht Club was originally organized as part of the *New York Tribune*'s development. By 1920 the club members had a fleet of sneakboxes with varied sail colors, lending the club its original name, Polyhue, whose members also contributed boats to the other classes, including catboats and sloops.

In 1933, with hard times affecting Beachwood residents as well as the rest of the country, the yacht club was dissolved. The building was signed over to the Beachwood Property Owners Association, and eventually to the Borough of Beachwood. Polyhue's members disbanded, although they kept sailing and entertaining from their homes and the beach.

In 1939, the old yacht club building was restored and the Beachwood Commissioners proposed a race to promote sailing. Junior sailing was encouraged, and a sailing-based social scene developed around the club. In 1947 Beachwood Yacht Club was officially reborn. A fire in 1978 resulted in the BYC having to leave the Community Club, and a couple of trailers became the official clubhouse until May 1981, when the new clubhouse was built and dedicated.

The current home of the Beachwood Yacht Club was inspired by the original 1920s Polyhue Yacht Club.

It is interesting that the Island Heights boats have the best start off their hometown club. Perhaps the crowd on the dock inspired the aggression demonstrated by IH L and IH 1.

Island Heights Yacht Club became a member of the Barnegat Bay Yacht Racing Association in 1914, the same year it was founded. The club has traditionally sponsored the 4th of July races, and has a proud history of yachting on the bay. Members include national champions and Olympians, and the club hosts many local, regional, and national regattas in several classes.

ISLAND HEIGHTS
Yacht Club

The Island Heights Yacht Club was first organized at a meeting of about thirty summer residents on July 28, 1898. By the next month, by-laws and a constitution were adopted, the stated objectives of the club being "to promote yachting and rowing, and to foster athletic sports upon the water," reflecting both the interest in physical culture of the time, and the growing appreciation for the boating possibilities on Barnegat Bay. Dues were assessed for men only, but women could join as "ladies auxiliary members" in 1899.

The unique IHYC clubhouse, constructed on pilings in the river, was ready for the summer of 1900, and interclub races with the yacht clubs of Bay Head and Seaside Park were instituted. Spectators often went to these races by chartered trains. Today, IHYC also supports a large enclosed marina for its larger racing auxiliary fleet, an extremely active fleet that races all summer on a down bay course.

While the emphasis is on yacht racing, IHYC also provides an active social calendar for its members. IHYC organized its junior sailing program in the 1950s with the purchase of 20 Clarke duckboats. This fleet was replaced with Parrine-built diamonds, which in turn were replaced with David Beaton's duckboats. A Cats compete for the Rodman Wanamaker Trophy, the Lostrom Cup, and the J. Willard Morgan Cup.

Lavallette Yacht Club was one of the original six clubs in the Barnegat Bay Yacht Racing Association, formed in 1914. In the 1920s and early '30s, when 50 to 60 sneakboxes from eight clubs raced in BBYRA's weekly regattas, Lavallette skippers won several Bay Championships. Three of the original five historic A Cats have represented Lavallette at one time or another, and all brought championships back to the club. A Cats compete each year for the Newman Trophy at the Lavallette Yacht Club BBYRA race.

The sail letter designations looks like bad Scrabble.

Newman Trophy

Year	Boat	Year	Boat	Year	Boat
2005	No Race	1997–2000	Ghost	1992	Bat
2004	Raven	1996	Vapor	1991	Wasp
2003	Torch	1995	Spy	1990	Mary Ann
2002	Witch	1994	Ghost	1987–1989	Spy
2001	Spy II	1993	Wasp		

2005: no racing

LAVALLETTE
Yacht Club

The Lavallette Yacht Club was born at a convocation of the R to R (Road to Ruin) resort on August 13, 1904. The original clubhouse was built on the oceanfront, not the bayside, taking good advantage of the cooler, more pleasant ocean breezes.

In 1906, Commodore Charles C. Eareckson donated land at President Avenue on the bay to satisfy the members who were interested in sailing, gunning, and fishing, rather than just the social aspects of life on the oceanside.

The bird in the foreground seems to be walking on the water in front of the Lavallette Yacht Club.

By the 1948 season, the clubhouse itself had been relocated to its current location, on Swan Point, and the club has seen good growth ever since. There is a waiting list for new members, and the club has a comprehensive junior sailing program; a training fleet; and its own tow, committee, and patrol boats.

These A Cat sailors are not fazed by the squall passing through.

Boating and racing—sailboats and powerboats—as well as tennis and socializing were the heart of the Manasquan River Yacht Club from the beginning. Admitted to BBYRA in 1962, MRYC has distinguished itself as "down bay" ever since, as evidenced by the wheels of Bay Championship flags displayed in the main deck of the clubhouse.

MANASQUAN RIVER
Yacht Club

The Manasquan River Yacht Club in Brielle, New Jersey, was founded in the fall of 1899 by a group of 16 men. Half were summer residents, businessmen from northern New Jersey and New York City, and half were local residents whose livelihoods depended on the sea or seasonal resort trade. They shared a common passion for sailing.

Manasquan River Yacht Club is the northernmost club in the BBYRA. The building was constructed in 1962.

During the first summer season of 1900, MRYC membership numbered 85. The clubhouse was a former ice cream parlor/cyclist stop, rented from charter member Capt. T.S.P. Brown. MRYC moved to its present location in 1907, where a new clubhouse was built incorporating the ice cream pavilion, which had been moved to the site.

When the current clubhouse was completed in 1962, it marked the beginning of year-round club life.

The most exciting place to watch a race is at the leeward mark. This rounding appears to be close.

The Mantoloking Yacht Club has a proud history of sailing, and a long list of sailing awards and achievements. These started with the early days of free-for-all catboat racing, and included local classes such as the 20-foot sneakbox class of the teens and twenties, and the 15-foot Perrine and Beaton sneakboxes. Mantoloking sailors—both men and women—have gone on to win national, international, and world championships, including providing the U.S. with 10 Olympians. The Louise Edgar Colie Trophy is awarded each year to the A Cat winner for the Mantoloking Yacht Club BBYRA race. The trophy was donated in honor of her 100th birthday in 1991.

MANTOLOKING
Yacht Club

The history of the Mantoloking Yacht Club indicates the date of its origin is 1897, when the original club was formed as the Mantoloking Golf Club. The golf course wandered from the dunes to the bay and was played with an easily identifiable red ball.

In 1900, with sailing growing on the bay, the club expanded its focus and changed its name to the Mantoloking Golf and Yacht Club, with a newly constructed clubhouse by the bay. On July 3, 1907, the name was finally changed to the Mantoloking Yacht Club. The Downers, who were the founding family of Mantoloking, donated the land for the yacht club. The original clubhouse is preserved, as it constitutes the southern part of the present building. The Downer Sailing Center was dedicated on the property in 1995 to honor several members of the Downer family.

The Mantoloking Yacht Club has produced 10 Olympic sailors.

Ten A Cats tied up to the outer dock at Metedeconk River Yacht Club. Richard Yetman's powerboat, Fin, *has secured the pole position along with the MRYC launches.*

Metedeconk River Yacht Club provides a very extensive sailing calendar for its members and other competitors, encouraging all sailors, whether they are sailing Sunfish or one-designs with the latest and greatest gear, to get out on the bay. MRYC is home to racing almost five days a week, six months of the year, which means there's something happening almost every weekday from May through October. But the season change doesn't end the club's activities on the bay; there is also an active frostbite fleet, and even a few ice boats for the really cold-weather enthusiasts.

METEDECONK RIVER
Yacht Club

Founded in 1936 by a group of devoted yachtsmen, Metedeconk River Yacht Club was organized around the twin principles of advancing the sport of yachting, and promoting the social enjoyment and good fellowship of its members.

The club was originally situated in a small boathouse on the north side of the Metedeconk River. By 1963, membership had grown sufficiently that the founders of the club could purchase adequate land across the river, at MRYC's present site.

This property was improved for the use of the sailing-oriented club by the installation of a bulkhead, docks, and a slip area. A main clubhouse was also built, and has been added onto three times, the latest addition having been accomplished in 2001. Swimming is also a focus at MRYC, and an inground pool was added in 1972, subsequently graced by its own poolhouse.

The new clubhouse was dedicated in 2001.

The club fosters an extensive junior sailing program as well as a junior swimming program, and from June through August, there are daily classes and competitions, regattas and races for the junior members. Enthusiasm, on the dock and around the pool, is high.

A perfect day. July 9, 2005 on Green Island racecourse off Normandy Beach Yacht Club.

Over the winter of 1998–1999, the old Normandy Beach Yacht Club was renovated by Commodore Arthur Manns Harden. It provides a beautiful home for the sailing activities, including a strong junior sailing program and races for prestigious trophies.

NORMANDY BEACH
Yacht Club

Normandy Beach Yacht Club was formed in 1945 as the Normandy Beach Sailing Club. At that time, Sunday races were held from the north side of Harbor Court, which was just a bayberry-covered peninsula with one house on it. A second house was built within a year, on the starting line, but club activities continued to be centered around the spot for a period of time. Interest in sailing increased rapidly, and it became fashionable to serve cocktails after the last gun was fired. Social activity flourished, and soon increasing attendance indicated the need for a more formalized group. Along with that came the need for land and a clubhouse.

In 1955, Normandy Beach Yacht Club raised funds to purchase land and water rights, and over three years the present clubhouse was constructed.

Normandy Beach Yacht Club.

Ocean Gate Yacht Club was one of four Barnegat Bay yacht clubs first involved with the organization of the Barnegat Bay Yacht Racing Association in 1914. Its participation in, and involvement with, the BBYRA through the years has persisted, and now up to three generations of OGYC members have enjoyed access to and competitive sport upon the bay as members of Ocean Gate. A Cats compete for the Beck Crabbe Trophy each year.

Crews hoist mainsails at the start of the Beck Crabbe Trophy race off Ocean Gate. Hoisting the main and hauling in the anchor simultaneously must be done with great care. This unique start is always a favorite for spectators.

Beck Crabbe Trophy

Year	Boat	Year	Boat
2005	*Witch*	2003	*Spy II*
2004	*Ghost*	2002	*Torch*

OCEAN GATE
Yacht Club

The Ocean Gate Yacht Club was founded in 1909 by a group of summer residents from Philadelphia, "to promote yachting and rowing and foster athletic sports upon the water." As the community grew, so did the scope of OGYC's purpose, which expanded to include an active social program for its members and their guests. The Board of Governors met throughout the season, and also through the winter in Philadelphia, with sharp eyes for the future of OGYC.

The original clubhouse was completed in 1912. Accessed by a long catwalk or by boat, the building holds a main room with two fireplaces and a kitchen. This building has grown and gone through many changes, including having a stage attached to the west side in the 1920s.

By the 1980s the original clubhouse had become structurally unsound, and a major rebuilding project was undertaken. In 1994, the present clubhouse was dedicated, complete with protective breakwater, bulkhead, and docks more appropriate to the look of the club and the modern needs of the sailors.

Snapper Applegate

There was the time Mike Frankovich T-boned my boat at anchor, during an anchor start at Ocean Gate.

My mom was on board as a matter of fact. I think she was 83 or 84 at the time. Mike always brought her aboard as a good luck charm. She just kind of sat there. Didn't do too much. But when the gun went off, being on the inside position, they got the sail up. They had a full head of steam going and the board was down just a little too far by the time they got to the sandbar.

Obviously everything just kind of went downhill from there. Mike proceeded. He's trying to get the boat under control, get the board up and everything. He got moving again but they didn't have enough momentum to keep her headed towards deeper water. I'm standing on my front porch, which overlooks the yacht club area, and I see Mike getting into trouble. And he is heading right for my Mako that is anchored out in front of my house. He tagged her amidships.

Makos are built pretty well. There is not much skeg on them so she took the shot pretty well. From what I hear from Michael, my mom was saying to Mike, "You're going to hit Snapper's boat! You're going to hit Snapper's boat!" And finally—boom— he did. This was when he was sailing *Bat*. She proceeded up onto the beach.

They got *Bat's* bow pointed back out off the beach, and they got back on the boat and they just sailed out. Headed for my boat again. Luckily they missed it on the second pass on their way out from the beach. I was just sitting there, watching from my deck. There is a movie of it around somewhere. Mike and I talk about that all the time.

Dan Crabbe

I like the race you start from anchor off Ocean Gate. They used to race down to what is now the Captain's Inn, used to be called Eno's. I can remember actually sailing through the old railroad bridge that went across between Seaside and Good Luck Point. And then anchoring and all going in for

Lasers and optimist dinghies prepare for racing at Ocean Gate Yacht Club.

The race starts with anchors down. Sails down. Gun goes off and all hell breaks loose. It is pretty hard getting your anchor up, getting your sail up, getting away, with 10 or 12 boats on the line. It's just a little hard not to bump somebody. —Peter Kellogg

a dinner at Eno's. The losing crews would always pay for the winner. That was a tradition I would like to see started again, or at least try it one time anyway. That was fun to do.

Peter Kellogg

I think one of the most fun things about the A Cat fleet is the "start from anchor" race. We call that "the boat builders mid-season work" job. I mean it is a little hard to get off that starting line without a little bit of bumping going on. It's a traditional

Ocean Gate race in honor of Beck Crabbe who was killed in a duck-hunting accident.

The plan is to be 50 feet, or two boatlengths apart, but I'm sure it is not the rule, because you anchor and everybody keeps on drifting. It is a little hard to tell how far apart the boats are. And it's hard to get up momentum with no jib to help swing the bow around. So it is a little interesting at times. And the nice part about it is there's always a lot of "friendly animation" between the crews. Lots of baloney going on.

A Cats off Good Luck Point head for the leeward mark. All boats are reefed for the next upwind leg.

An associate member of the BBYRA since 1949, full membership was granted to Pine Beach Yacht Club in 1980. Since then, the sailing prowess of both senior and junior members has made the club a more formidable contender in both one-design and auxiliary racing. The junior sailing program, started in 1975, has brought both honor and fame to the club. Of all the club's activities, perhaps none has brought more recognition than the champion performance of Pine Beach Yacht Club junior sailors in BBYRA and interclub races, both through excellence on the racecourse and all-around good sportsmanship.

PINE BEACH
Yacht Club

In 1910, Charles F. Wheeler and William Wilson, early residents of Pine Beach, decided there was a need for a clubhouse. By May 1916 they had sold enough shares to incorporate the Pine Beach Yacht Club, for "the promotion and enjoyment of yachting, fishing and gunning, and general social purposes." The clubhouse opened in August on the Toms River, only to be greatly expanded five years later, as membership and activity at PBYC grew. Sailboat racing was initiated in 1944 with a popular series of Sunday races, and the club was always the social hub of Pine Beach.

The clubhouse itself has served as an election hall, police station, tea room, dining hall, theater, and snack bar—as well as a recreation and sailing school for youngsters, a breeding ground for champion racers, and an important member of the Barnegat Bay racing cohort.

Junior sailing lessons get underway at Pine Beach Yacht Club.

Compare this scene at Seaside Park Yacht Club with the historical photograph on page eight.

Seaside Park Yacht Club holds a special place in the hearts of BBYRA sailors who traditionally wrap up the "official" sailing season on the SPYC course over Labor Day weekend. The Sewell and Middleton Cups are coveted by A Cats each year.

SEASIDE PARK
Yacht Club

Seaside Park Yacht Club evolved from some of the earliest races and regattas on Barnegat Bay. In the 1890s, Mr. Henry J. West offered large cash prizes for sneakbox races on the bay. These races started at the present public dock, went on to Westray's Point, to the drawbridge, then back to the public dock, four laps. Heavy participation came from the lifeguards working at the beaches.

The formation of an American Sneakbox Owners Association was suggested during an 1899 meeting held in the basement of Mr. West's (and later SPYC Commodore Wolstenholme's) cottage at the corner of 5th Avenue and the bay. Later that year, a convocation of all cottage owners and yachtsmen was held at the home of John Weaver, resulting in the formation of the Seaside Park Yacht Club. Mr. Weaver was elected commodore. The clubhouse was soon built, and soon expanded, as boating boomed to an unprecedented degree. Development of the area brought with it enthusiastic sailors and competition was keen. SPYC, with its famous fleet of racing yachts, swept the honors. All along the Atlantic Seaboard, Barnegat Bay became known as the home of the world's fastest catboats. The social program at SPYC, and its delightful clubhouse, continue a tradition of providing land-based entertainment and activities to compliment the sailing.

Bob Engle, former commodore of Island Heights Yacht Club

We were sailing in the Seaside Park A Cat race. The year was 1951 or 1952. The wind was strong out of the northwest, which is different from what we had had all summer, so it was like sailing on a new body of water.

I was sailing aboard the *Bat*. On the downwind leg heading back toward SPYC, we were running in second place. We noticed in a particularly strong puff of wind that the boat ahead decided to go through a tack instead of a jibe. For us on *Bat* it was our big chance to catch up with a jibe. My job on the boat was trimming the main. So I coiled up the line to be prepared for the maneuver. When the boom swung across, the line actually smoked through the blocks. It was impressive. Somehow the *Bat* survived the maneuver but the image is still in my mind after over 50 years. The move was successful, and we went on to win that particular race.

At the same regatta, Runnie Colie had a big lead in the E Scow class. We noticed that suddenly his mainsail went down. All the other boats were well behind but caught up.

Suddenly the mainsail on Colie's boat was hauled to the top of the mast and he tacked his E Scow away for another mark. Apparently he'd been heading for the wrong mark and was afraid to alter course because the other boats behind would cut the corner and pass him. So it was a slight of hand to trick the fleet to stay in the lead. What a cagy sailor Runnie is.

The Sewell Cup and Middleton Cup.

The final race of the BBYRA is traditionally held at the Seaside Park Yacht Club.

Middleton Cup

2005	Ghost	1986–1987	Bat	1970	Mary Ann	1946–1947	Spy
2004	Raven	1985	Spy	1969	Lotus	1941	Bat
2002–2003	Ghost	1982–1984	Wasp	1967–1968	Mary Ann	1940	Lotus
2000	Ghost	1981	Mary Ann	1965–1966	Spy	1939	Mary Ann
1999	Wasp	1980	Bat	1963	Spy	1938	Tamwock
1997–1998	Ghost	1979	Mary Ann	1962	Bat	1937	Lotus
1996	Vapor	1978	Bat	1961	Lotus	1936	Tamwock
1995	Mary Ann	1977	Lotus	1960	Mary Ann	1932–1935	Mary Ann
1994	Ghost	1976	Spy	1957–1959	Lotus	1929–1931	Lotus
1992–1993	Mary Ann	1975	Bat	1956	Mary Ann	1927–1928	Bat
1991	Bat	1974	Spy	1953–1955	Lotus	1923–1924	Mary Ann
1989–1990	Spy	1972–1973	Bat	1950	Spy		
1988	Wasp	1971	Lotus	1948–1949	Bat		

1925, 1926, 1942–1945, 1951, 1952, 1964, 2001: no racing

Sewell Cup

2005	Witch	1984	Wasp	1962	Spy	1935	Wasp
2004	Raven	1983	Mary Ann	1961	Bat	1934	Bat
2003	Vapor	1982	Wasp	1959–1960	Spy	1933	Wasp
2002	Torch	1981	Mary Ann	1957–1958	Lotus	1932	Bat
2001	Spy II	1978–1980	Bat	1956	Spy	1930–1931	Tamwock
1997–2000	Ghost	1977	Lotus	1953–1955	Lotus	1929	Spy
1996	Mary Ann	1976	Spy	1952	Spy	1928	Tamwock
1995	Vapor	1972–1975	Bat	1951	Lotus	1927	Spy
1994	Ghost	1971	Mary Ann	1950	Spy	1926	Tamwock
1993	Wasp	1970	Bat	1946–1949	Bat	1925	Lotus
1992	Mary Ann	1969	Spy	1941	Lotus	1924	Spy
1991	Wasp	1968	Mary Ann	1939–1940	Bat	1922–1923	Mary Ann
1988–1989	Wasp	1965–1967	Spy	1938	Tamwock		
1986–1987	Bat	1964	Mary Ann	1937	Bat		
1985	Spy	1963	Bat	1936	Lotus		

1942–1945, 1990: no racing

So eager to be racing were the Shore Acres Yacht Club members that the first sailboat races were held less than a year after the club was founded, on June 28, 1941, and a week before the clubhouse was officially opened. SAYC became a member of the Barnegat Bay Yacht Racing Association the following year, and hosted its first BBYRA regatta. Junior sailing had its start with a program initiated in the '60s and early '70s, and in 1994, SAYC started a new junior sailing program in the world-renowned Optimist pram. The Scorers Cup was donated by Don Turner in 1993 for the winner of the BBYRA A Cat race hosted by Shore Acres Yacht Club.

Don Turner donated the Scorers Cup in 1993 in honor of the many people who score races.

Scorers Cup

Year	Boat	Year	Boat	Year	Boat	Year	Boat
2005	*Lightning*	2001	*Raven*	1998	*Wasp*	1994	*Ghost*
2003	*Raven*	2000	*Ghost*	1997	*Ghost*	1993	*Wasp*
2002	*Witch*	1999	*Ghost*	1995	*Tamwock*		

1996, 2004: no racing

SHORE ACRES
Yacht Club

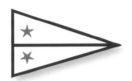

Shore Acres began as a pioneer land development community in the 1930s, marketed as the "Venice" of the Jersey Shore. Ten years later the Shore Acres Yacht Club held its first members' meeting. Records show that there were 33 active members, defined as a male, over the age of 21. All others were classified as Flag Members, and enjoyed reduced dues and fees.

The clubhouse was built on what SAYC members believe is the best location on Barnegat Bay, and was formally opened on July 4, 1941. The original clubhouse had many small rooms, a fireplace, piano, jukebox, and pinball machine. SAYC was a center for social camaraderie as well as for boating, and the traditional Friday and Saturday night dinners, parties, and Sunday lunches held in conjunction with the Sunday races have all contributed to lasting friendships and affection for the club.

Shore Acres Yacht Club.

Spy II *wins the Toms River Challenge Cup in 2003.*

Toms River Yacht Club joined the Barnegat Bay Yacht Racing Association in 1922, and was from the first a strong participant in organized racing on Barnegat Bay, as it continues to be today. In that same year the first A Cat was built specifically to win the Toms River Challenge Cup.

TOMS RIVER
Yacht Club

The Toms River Yacht Club was formally organized on July 1, 1871. Just 25 days later, the club sponsored its first regatta: a race for a unique silver trophy, donated by its designer, Joseph Chattelier, a charter member of the club. This trophy was created by Tiffany & Company at a cost of $175, and at the time, was raced for twice a year. As it has been the prize in regular sailing competitions continuously since its introduction, the Toms River Challenge Cup is the second oldest perpetual racing trophy in the United States, second only to the America's Cup currently held by Switzerland. The trophy resides in the club trophy case for all to admire.

The club was leased to the U.S. Coast Guard Auxiliary during World War II. This, combined with successful fundraising projects and the fact that the members and their families worked at dinners, dances, and parties, insured the continuation and improvement of the club.

Twenty junior sailors discover the joy of A Cat sailing in the summer of 2005.

A newly constructed clubhouse was dedicated in 1968, and four years later the Money Island Yacht Club merged with the TRYC, providing the TRYC with additional property as well as additional enthusiastic, experienced sailor–members. The club has since expanded, insuring adequate facilities for now and the future.

Toms River Yacht Club is proud to be the home club for many nationally and internationally renowned sailors, and continues its commitment to promote friendly competition and interest in activities connected to sailing, boating, and yachting.

Gary Stewart

I'm embarrassed to say this, but I count the days to the Challenge Cup every year. To me it is the most important race of the year, even though they all count the same. It is the reason these boats were built. The *Mary Ann* was built simply to win the Challenge Cup.

Toms River Challenge Cup victory pennant.

The first time I won it, I just couldn't believe it. I've got a picture in my office of my daughter, she was two years old then, kissing the Challenge Cup.

Mike Frankovich

I'd say probably one of the coolest things is winning the Toms River Challenge Cup. That is just so historic. We actually did that once with the *Bat*. And that was really a fond moment.

Woogie Law

During the 100th anniversary race for the Toms River Challenge Cup I was in third place at the last mark. I had not won a race all year. *Spy* and *Lotus* took the last mark to starboard, which I knew was wrong. I protested both of them. They were disqualified and

I won the 100th anniversary race of the Challenge Cup. The Sayias would not talk to me for three months after that race.

The Toms River Challenge Cup.

The oldest continuously held sailing trophy in the United States is hosted by the Toms River Yacht Club.

Toms River Challenge Cup

2005	*Witch*	1986	*Spy*	1967	*Mary Ann*	1941	*Bat*
2004	*Raven*	1985	*Wasp*	1966	*Spy*	1940	*Lotus*
2001–2003	*Spy II*	1984	*Spy*	1964–1965	*Mary Ann*	1939	*Bat*
2000	*Ghost*	1983	*Wasp*	1963	*Spy*	1938	*Mary Ann*
1998–1999	*Vapor*	1981–1982	*Mary Ann*	1962	*Bat*	1934–1937	*Lotus*
1996–1997	*Mary Ann*	1980	*Bat*	1959–1961	*Mary Ann*	1931–1933	*Bat*
1995	*Ghost*	1979	*Mary Ann*	1955–1958	*Lotus*	1930	*Lotus*
1993	*Bat*	1978	*Bat*	1953–1954	*Bat*	1929	*Bat*
1992	*Wasp*	1974–1977	*Spy*	1950–1952	*Spy*	1928	*Tamwock*
1991	*Spy*	1972–1973	*Bat*	1948–1949	*Bat*	1926–1927	*Spy*
1990	*Wasp*	1970–1971	*Mary Ann*	1947	*Mary Ann*	1925	*Bat*
1988–1989	*Spy*	1968–1969	*Lotus*	1946	*Bat*	1922–1924	*Mary Ann*
1987	*Bat*	*1942–1945, 1994: no racing*					

Challenge Cup races between 1871 and 1922 were not sailed on A Cats. The first boat to win in 1871 was named Vapor.

Interesting that each boat is sailing a slightly different course on this puffy day. The scariest job is sitting on the boom with your feet off the deck.

A DAY ON THE BAY

The crew of Spy *had a good day on the Green Island course.*

"We sure have a lot of helm," were my first words after heading up on the wind aboard *Spy*. Roy Wilkins, Gary Stewart, and Richard Yetman all laughed, "Welcome back to the A Cat!"

It had been 36 years since I'd last sailed on an A Cat. In the process of interviewing the owners and builders, studying the history of the class, and selecting the best photographs, I became very curious; what are A Cats like to steer? I had never done it. My chance finally arrived on week three of the 2005 BBYRA summer series. We were up bay on the Green Island course for a day hosted by the Mantoloking Yacht Club.

On *Spy* we were first to hoist our sails. Regular helmsman Gary Stewart, dressed for the occasion in a bowtie, gave me the tiller. I promised him the use of my Laser in Annapolis in return. The mainsail looked huge, the boat very wide. The wooden boat smells made me smile, thinking back to my father's Atlantic City catboat named *The African Queen*. And the water gurgling in the centerboard trunk was just as mysterious as I remembered.

All 10 A Cats had top-notch helmsmen, but the real MVP on board was the mainsail trimmer, Richard Yetman. I told him he was my new best friend. The "main man" can make or break the helmsman and the two have to be in sync to sail an A Cat efficiently.

Thomas A. Mathis Causeway. Dedicated on May 24, 1950 to coincide with the 100th anniversary of the founding of Ocean County, it was named in honor of an Ocean County former senator. Fin *tows* Spy *up bay.*

Gary Jobson at the helm of Spy *on July 9, 2005. Steering an A Cat gives you a sense of purpose and power.*

Stewart served as tactician. I think he liked looking around for a change, as the helmsman has to be extremely focused. The sailing characteristics of an A Cat are remarkably similar to those of the 12-meter boats: both are mainsail-oriented boats, and they do not like to be over-powered, are slow to maneuver, and are raced by very motivated owners.

Mid-deck crew Maggie Groff and Jane Wilkins frequently jumped off the rail to tend to many adjustments above and below the deck. Both women had smiles all day. The seventh member of our crew, Tyler Yetman, 16, served as the human boom vang. I had the same job 45 years ago.

Before the start, a rival boat came alongside us, questioning my eligibility to steer. I pointed out that I was a member of both Beachwood and Toms River Yacht Clubs. I overheard someone on our boat mutter "up bay people!" I knew then the other boats would be gunning for us.

Witch, Lightning, *and* Spy *get off to a fast start.*

Just before the preparatory signal was sounded, several boats started shaking their reefed mainsails out. The wind was dying. As the seconds ticked down Gary Stewart liked the port end and we went for it. Steering an A Cat is hard work. They feel tight, like a luxury car. Maneuvering must be planned early and performed with great care, but I found that each adjustment made a difference in speed. It made me wonder if two of these boats ever went out and formally speed tested. One would learn a lot from experimenting.

The Sewell Cup started in 1904. When A Cats started racing for this trophy in 1922, Mary Ann won it the first two years.

The boats seem fairly even in speed. Tactics proved to be the difference on this day and it was apparent that Roy knows his stuff. It was helpful to minimize tacks and jibes. E Scows, Lightnings, Sanderlings and Flying Scots racing on the same course gave us clues about the next puff, as the westerly wind varied between 7 and 20 knots and shifted through 60 degrees. Every sailor on the water was intense. We finished second. The winner, a few boatlengths ahead, was *Lightning*. Our crew cheered mightily for them. What a nice moment for everyone, I thought.

It wasn't long before the second race got underway. *Spy* was at the Race Committee boat end at the gun and our position looked good, but then the wind shifted hard to port. Suddenly we were fifth and stayed that way to the finish. It was quiet on *Spy*. Then as we crossed the line our crew jumped up spontaneously and congratulated each other on a great day. Indeed!

On the three-hour car ride back to Annapolis, as thunderstorms loomed on the horizon, I reflected on the day and the A Cat class. Listening to the rivalries I think an Up Bay vs. Down Bay Team Race should be established.

It is also apparent that these boats need to be preserved. In a heartwarming way the A Cats connect the generations. If every boat was required to include at least one sailor under 16 years of age, it would help inspire juniors, and keep the class going in future years.

Sunset on the Toms River.

The Spy *received this red flag for second place, July 9, 2005.*

The concept of adhering to class rules and traditional designs is to be applauded and continued. Nelson Hartranft and Lolly Beaton were correct to encourage new construction to keep wooden boat–building skills alive. Racing an A Cat is a big commitment, but the class epitomizes the very fabric of a magic sailing area and the good-spirited sailors of the Jersey Shore.

—Gary Jobson

OCEAN COUNTY COLLEGE

Painting by Ken Bernhardt.

Ocean County College was founded in 1964 as the first community college in New Jersey. There are more than 8,000 students taking classes at the college, most of whom complete their core requirements and then transfer to four-year institutions.

President Dr. Jon Larson's commitment to ensuring that the college represented its unique seacoast/sailing environment led to a meeting in 2001 with A Cat sailor and fleet captain, Roy Wilkins, and dean of students, Don Doran. Jon challenged Roy and Don to create a collegiate sailing program within one year. His charge was simple, "Barnegat Bay is home to a talented pool of junior sailors. We want to offer an opportunity for them to continue their development as competitive collegiate sailors and get a first-class education close to home." Dr. Drew F. Seibert assembled and chaired a "blue ribbon" sailing advisory board that now guides the development of the program, and is the foundation of the program's sailing and fundraising success.

From an initial purchase of six 420 class boats, in four short years the OCC program has grown to include sixteen sailors with nineteen 420s, four FJs, and two patrol boats. The program has formed a partnership with Monmouth University to coach and manage their intercollegiate sailing program. Their students now practice with OCC students as well as seven area high school teams, which are growing as a result of the easy access to OCC's boats and coaching staff. A key component of the OCC program has been the continued development of the junior sailing talent along Barnegat Bay. Many students "age out" of the yacht club junior programs at age 16. The collegiate program encourages these students to continue sailing in their junior and senior year for their respective high schools, and provides natural recruitment opportunities for the Ocean and Monmouth sailing programs.

The OCC sailing team before a practice at IHYC, spring 2005.

The Ocean County College sailing program is a model of private cooperation and generosity for the public good and the advancement of sailing. It is a tale of the power of community cooperation and leadership. Successful sailing, coaching, race management, and academic achievement are the core of the Ocean County College program. Collegiate sailors are treated as first-class athletes. Most importantly, OCC collegiate sailors receive a quality education from a team of dedicated faculty and staff who see each student as unique and capable of great achievements.

The future for the program is quite exciting. Ocean County College is a partner with the Toms River Seaport Society under the leadership of Mr. Bob O'Brien. This partnership has created the

Ocean County College is one of the most competitive teams in the middle Atlantic Intercollegiate District. Start of 2005 OCC Spring Open with 19 colleges at Toms River Yacht Club. OCC won the regatta.

Barnegat Bay Sailing Hall of Fame to honor the great sailing talent that the region has produced for generations. The Hall of Fame held its first induction ceremony in September 2004 at the college. Sail-Habilitation, under the leadership of Dr. Stephanie Argyris, is a partner with the program. Sail-Habilitation encourages the use of sailing in the rehabilitation of the physically challenged. In addition, the OCC sailing program is now a partner with the Barnegat Bay Yacht Racing Association in promoting race management and sailing seminars, and with the Nelson School of Sailing in Island Heights in providing community sailing classes to area residents. The college is also working in partnership with the

The Luce Trophy, won by Ocean County College in 2002 and 2003.

Ocean County Board of Freeholders to build a sailing center at a county park with private donations. This center will serve as a home for the sailing club, its boats, and equipment.

The college is very proud of the achievements of the sailing program. It has helped to foster the Barnegat Bay region as a center for sailing education, competition, and excellence. Its continued success is dependent on tapping the rich talent and resources of the area and guiding them for the common goal of the advancement of sailing. Dr. Larson states, "We have some high aspirations, including a new sailing center, a community sailing program, a program for the disabled, and new academic programs in clean marina management, marine science, and coastal area environmental management." If the past four years are any indication, the future course of sailing on Barnegat Bay is a winning one.

Drew Seibert

Ocean County College uses an A Cat for a management training seminar on

Drew Seibert

the water, with people who basically have never sailed before, to teach the idea of teamwork. It has been a good drill for the college to get some of the professors to work together.

Gary Jobson

I was standing at the water's edge on the Toms River during Ocean County College's spring practice with volunteer chairman Drew Seibert. It was a blustery day and a great vantage point.

You could see every action that affected the boats while standing close by. It is no accident that college football and basketball coaches stand right on the sideline to get the feel of the game.

By my eye, the Ocean County sailors were getting a good workout. Seibert liked what he saw too. On-the-water race manager Roy Wilkins, who is actually a long-time soccer coach, directed the activity. The sailors went through repetitive drills, practice starts, and races. Little time was wasted rotating boats. The sun was dipping the horizon quickly and everyone wanted to make the most of the day. The following weekend Ocean County College would enter its freshmen and sophomores against four-year programs in a hotly contested event on the Chesapeake. On the one hand, community sailors are at a disadvantage

The Ocean County College team aboard Spy *with coach Roy Wilkins (r).*

because they are younger. But on the other hand they don't have to wait to make the starting squad. Those that transfer to a four-year college have a clear head start beginning in their junior year.

The rapid progress made by the appropriately named Ocean County College serves as an excellent example of what a junior college can do in a short period of time. Jon Larson, president of Ocean County College, wanted to offer junior sailors an opportunity to continue their development as competitive collegiate sailors and get a first-class education close to home.

Roy Wilkins was inspired by an article written by *Cruising World* editor Herb McCormick in the *The New York Times* about the high level of talent emerging from the New Jersey Shore. Over the last three years on the All-Jobson Juniors list, 13 out of 33 junior sailors have been from New Jersey.

Crewmember being recovered aboard Tamwock *during an OCC team-building session. The entire crew had a good laugh but it looks serious at this moment.*

To get a program off the ground takes dedicated support from the top. Ocean County College President Jon Larson points out, "OCC is the only community college with an intercollegiate sailing program on the East Coast. I like the company this puts us in. Sailing competitively against Navy, St. Mary's, Princeton, and other MAISA universities makes a statement about OCC . . . this is an exceptional institution and we want people to know it."

These kinds of programs don't happen automatically. Everyone I talked to in Toms River was quick to emphasize the strong support of local yacht clubs, including Island Heights Yacht Club and Toms River Yacht Club. The collective wisdom of Seibert's strong advisory committee has given OCC a fast start. "In order to build a sound program you need a strong synergy between the college, area yacht clubs (Island Heights Yacht Club and Toms River Yacht Club in our case), local marinas, civic organizations (Rotary Club, Elks Club, etc.) and philanthropic as well as political support from community leaders. In our case we could not have done it without this total support of so many hard-working and generous people."

During the summer months these clubs use Ocean County College's 420s for adult instruction and training. In addition, the Toms River Yacht Club recently purchased 30 used Tech dinghies from MIT. That is a lot of available equipment for a young team.

The junior college athletes are ecstatic. Matt Geotting, a sophomore and A team skipper for the past two years at Ocean County College says, "We've been lucky so far to have really committed kids who have been with the program for two years. We have an advantage because we get to sail and compete sooner, we do not have to wait for spots on the team to open up. This can be a disadvantage because we are usually going against a lot of juniors and seniors but so far we have been pretty competitive."

Christine Restivo, a sophomore from Toms River South High School who sailed for Beachwood Yacht Club, declares, "College sailing has been an incredible experience that involved a lot of hard work and has been tons of fun. I've been sailing since I was 10 years old so I really appreciate the opportunities collegiate sailing has given me to continue the sport. I will be attending Monmouth University in West Long Branch, New Jersey, in the fall and plan on participating in their sailing club."

When asked about how big a program he is looking to build, Roy Wilkins explains, "Our strategic plan calls for the development of the School of Seamanship and Sailing at Ocean County College, a regional provider of resources, education, and support for maritime interests. One part of the program is the Intercollegiate Competitive Team. This fall we will be hosting the MAISA (Middle Atlantic Intercollegiate Sailing Association) Clinic, the OCC Crossroads Realty Fall Open, and the OCC Sovereign Bank Club Championships."

Ocean County College has come a long way in a very short period of time. You can learn more about the program at www.ocean.edu. High school sailing has done well over the past 10 years and community college sailing is the next trend that could take our sport to higher levels.

Old Mantoloking Bridge. The first Mantoloking Bridge was built in 1883 at a cost of $4,000. This one was built in 1938 and construction for its replacement was started in December 2003.

BIBLIOGRAPHY

Books

Grayson, Stan. *Catboats*. Marblehead, Massachusetts: Devereux Books, 1996.

Kraft, Bayard Randolph. *Under Barnegat's Beam*. Prepared for Publication by George H. Eckhardt, Distributed by Appleton, Parsons & Co., Inc. 1960.

Merrick, Sam. *F. Slade Dale—The Life of His Choice*. Ocean County Historical Society, 1998.

Miller, Pauline S. *Ocean County: Four Centuries in the Making*. Ocean County Cultural & Heritage Commission, 2000.

The rooster flag is passed on to the winner of each weekly race. The winner of the last race of the season keeps the flag.

Schoettle, Edwin J. *Sailing Craft*. Including p. 366, *The Toms River Cup*, Edward Crabbe. New York: The Macmillan Company, 1937.

Stephens, William P. *Traditions and Memories of American Yachting*. WoodenBoat Publications, Inc., 1989.

Nathanael Greene Herreshoff, William Picard Stephens, Their Last Letters 1930–1938. Annotated by John W. Streeter. Herreshoff Marine Museum, 1988.

Star Boat Design and Development. Edited by David Bolles. "Francis Sweisguth, Designer and Developer of the Star."

Spy II *touches water for the first time.*

Articles

Anthony, Irvin. "The Cats with More than Nine Lives." *Yachting* (March 1965).

Barr, Wayne B. "Catboats on Upper Barnegat Bay." *The Catboat Association Bulletin*, 105 (1994).

Dickson, Glen "Barnegat Bay's Ageless A Cats." *Sailing World* (February 2005).

Edwards, Bill. "The Cats Are Back." *Asbury Park Press* (June 1990).

Hebert, James. "New Jersey's Fables Barnegat A-Cats are Rescued From Near Extinction." *Offshore* (1990). www.barnegatbayacat.com/offshore.html

McHugh, Bob. "A Rare Breed of Catboat has New Member of Fleet." *Asbury Park Press* (June 21, 1982).

Pawling, G. Patrick. "On The Water: These Cats Can Flat Out Run." *Atlantic City Press* (July 15, 2001).

Petty, George. "Barnegat Bay's A-Cats." *WoodenBoat* (January/February 1985).

——— "The A-Cats of Barnegat Bay." *WoodenBoat* (March/April 2003).

Savadove, Larry. Review of *The Closed Sea* by Kent Mountford. *The SandPiper* (June 12, 2002).

Zusman, Charles. "The Spy is Coming in From the Cold." *The Star Ledger* (April 28, 2005).

The Catboat Association Bulletin No. 65 (June 1981), No. 69 (November 1982), No. 80 (June 1986), No. 85 (Spring 1988), No. 97 (Winter 1992), No. 102 (Fall 1993), No. 105 (Fall 1994), No. 110 (Spring 1996), No. 117 (Fall 1998), No. 119 (Spring 1999), No. 123 (Fall 2000), No. 126 (Fall 2001).

Web Sites

"A Cat Facts." www.barnegatbayacat.com/facts

"History of Barnegat." www.bbyra.org/history.html

New Jersey Maritime History Theme Stories. www.nps.gov/neje/maritime.html

Ocean County Historical Museum Timeline. www.co.ocean.nj.us/museums/history.htm

Transcription of talk given by John Peter Brewer to the S.S. Crocker Association Annual Meeting, www.catboats.org/crocker.htm

The 1975 A Cat Championship flag won by Bat *out of Island Heights Yacht Club. Every BBYRA A Cat champion has received an identical flag since 1922.*

IMAGE CREDITS

Virginia Perle
paintings: cover and title page, pages 5, 97.
pen and inks: pages 101, 105, 109, 111, 115, 117, 119, 121, 123, 125, 129, 131, 135, 137.
photographs: pages 102–103.

RT Speck Photo
www.bayhead.com
table of contents page, pages vi, 20, 23 (bottom), 24, 25, 27, 28, 32, 48, 54, 58, 61, 62, 63 (bottom), 64, 66, 67, 68, 70 (top), 71, 72, 74, 76, 77, 78, 80 (bottom), 82 (top), 83 (top), 84, 86 (top), 87, 88, 90, 91, 92 (top), 93, 94, 96 (top), 114, 116, 118, 120, 122, 124, 127, 130, 136, 141.

Chetra E. Kotzas
BarnegatBayAcats.com
PhotographyKingdom.com
poem page, pages v, 4, 63 (top), 75, 80 (top), 81, 104, 106 (top), 107, 109, 112 (bottom), 113 (top), 115, 117, 119, 121, 123, 126, 128, 129, 132 (bottom), 134, 135, 139, 140, 147 (top), 150.

John English paintings: pages 1, 19.

Ken Bernhardt painting: page 145.

Barnegat Bay Water Estuary Foundation: pages 98–99 (for more information or to purchase go to www.bbwa.org).

A Cat Community: pages 6, 7, 8, 10, 11, 13, 18, 22, 26, 30, 31, 33, 34 (top), 35, 36, 38, 40, 42, 44 (both left), 45 (right), 47, 56, 57 (bottom), 70 (bottom), 106 (bottom), 144 (bottom), 152.

Jane Wilkins: inside cover, pages 43, 45 (left), 46, 86 (bottom), 148 (bottom).

Hartranft Collection: dedication page, page 57 (top).

Charlie Lord Collection: pages 2, 15, 16, 17.

Drew Seibert: pages 3, 142, 143 (top).

Schoettle Collection: pages 9, 12, 37, 51 (top).

Crabbe Collection: page 14.

Gale Yetman: page 23.

Arlene Lostrum Collection: page 34 (bottom).

Roy Wilkins: pages 44 (right), 60, 82 (bottom), 83 (bottom), 92 (bottom), 96 (bottom), 100, 112 (top), 113 (bottom), 138, 143 (bottom), 144 (top), 146, 147 (bottom), 151, 152 (bottom).

Brick Collection: pages 50, 51 (bottom), 52, 53.

Beachwood Yacht Club: page 108.

Fran Leigh: page 110.

Ed Vienckowski: page 132 (top).

Ocean County College: pages 148 (top), 149.

ACKNOWLEDGMENTS

Writing a book is a big task. In many ways writing a book is like racing a sailboat. It takes many people working together to get a good result.

We are grateful to the photographers and artists for their spectacular work. Especially Richard Speck and Chetra Kotzas. Richard Speck would like to thank Austin and Gwen Fragomen for the use of their boat to take these wonderful pictures. Virginia Perle's artwork jumps off the page. We are grateful for the use of the John English paintings on pages one and nineteen. And for Ken Bernhardt's painting on page 145.

Thanks to the Toms River Seaport Society for their extensive help providing information for the historical chapter. We are also most appreciative of the assistance by many members of the thirteen yacht clubs and the BBYRA. Thanks also to Kippy Requardt for her editing and research assistance.

We were quite fortunate to have the use of several historical collections of photographs including those of Charlie Lord, Alicemay Weber-Wright, the Schoettle family, Dan Crabbe and Steve Brick. Many other photos were provided by A Cat sailors throughout the Bay.

Thanks also to Ocean County College and President Dr. Jon Larson, Don Doran, and Dr. Dan Duffy. Also thanks to Bob O'Brien and Drew Seibert for their guidance throughout the project.

At Nomad Press, Susan Kahan worked tirelessly editing the copy and pulling all the material together, Sarah Torkelson managed the enormous library of images, and Jeff McAllister created an elegant design. Alex Kahan, publisher of Nomad Press, made the project a reality.

There are hundreds of pages of material from the interviews with over forty A Cat owners and sailors. This material has been given to the Toms River Seaport Society to keep in their archives.

During the production, Kathy Lambert looked after many details and collected endless amounts of information. Jane Wilkins offered many good ideas on editing content and layout. Thank you to Carol and Neil Titcomb of The Catboat Association for their assistance and providing archival material.